CONFRONTING
RELIGIOUS JUDGMENTALISM

A *Confronting Fundamentalism* Book

OTHER TITLES IN THIS SERIES:

Confronting Religious Denial of Gay Marriage
Confronting Religious Violence
Confronting Religious Denial of Science
Confronting Religious Absolutism
The Confrontational Wit of Jesus
Confronting a Controlling God

CONFRONTING RELIGIOUS JUDGMENTALISM

CHRISTIAN HUMANISM AND THE MORAL IMAGINATION

CATHERINE M. WALLACE

 CASCADE *Books* • Eugene, Oregon

CONFRONTING RELIGIOUS JUDGMENTALISM
Christian Humanism and the Moral Imagination

A Confronting Fundamentalism Book

Copyright © 2016 Catherine M. Wallace. All rights reserved. Except for brief quotations in critical publications or reviews, no part of this book may be reproduced in any manner without prior written permission from the publisher. Write: Permissions, Wipf and Stock Publishers, 199 W. 8th Ave., Suite 3, Eugene, OR 97401.

Cascade Books
An Imprint of Wipf and Stock Publishers
199 W. 8th Ave., Suite 3
Eugene, OR 97401

www.wipfandstock.com

ISBN 13: 978-1-4982-2890-9

Cataloging-in-Publication data

Wallace, Catherine M.

    Confronting religious judgmentalism: Christian humanism and the moral imagination / Catherine M. Wallace.

    xvi + 140 p. ; 21.5 cm. —Includes bibliographical references.

    Confronting Fundamentalism

    ISBN 13: 978-1-4982-2890-9

    1. Judgement (Ethics). 2. Religious right United States. I. Title.

BJ1408.5 .W20 2016

Manufactured in the U.S.A.

Excerpt from THE NEW JERUSALEM BIBLE, copyright © 1985 by Darton, Longman & Todd, Ltd. and Doubleday, a division of Random House, Inc. Reprinted by Permission.

Revised Standard Version of the Bible, copyright 1952 [2nd edition, 1971] by the Division of Christian Education of the National Council of the Churches of Christ in the United States of America. Used by permission. All rights reserved

*For Aislin Grace Wallace and Adelia Wren Wallace,
to whom the future belongs.*

Table of Contents

Preface ix

Acknowledgments xiii

1. Confronting Fundamentalism: It's Judgmental 1
2. 1998, 1968, 1970: *Just an Opinion* 9
3. Shame and the American Character 18
4. 1960: What the Sky Seemed to Say 30
5. Shame as a Moral Issue: The Forbidden Fruit 36
6. From Judgment to Judgmentalism: Some Quick History 48
7. Where Do We Look? 59
8. The Great Enlightenment Project 72
9. David Hume's Alternative: The Good Heart 82
10. How Do We Know? 89
11. Is This Heresy? 105
12. Conscience as a Creative Process 119
13: Postscript: What I Should Have Said to My Son 134

Bibliography 137

Preface

Thanks for picking up this book. After so many years of solitary work, it's thrilling to welcome a reader. I'm delighted you are here, and I hope you find what you are looking for. I look forward to hearing from you when you are finished reading. Please drop me a line at CatherineMWallace.com, follow me on Facebook, or on Twitter @Cate_Wallace.

This book stands on its own, completely self-contained. But I have written six similar books, each confronting a different aspect of hatemongering, hard-Right "Christianism." Think of them, perhaps, as other songs on the same album, an album titled *Confronting Fundamentalism*. But simply *confronting* fundamentalism is not enough. We also need a strong, religiously neutral language for moral values shared by the vast majority of Americans. To facilitate that conversation, I offer two useful concepts.

The first is *humanism*. Humanism is best defined as a pair of commitments. Morally, humanism is committed to the *humane* as an ethical standard. Intellectually, humanism is committed to critical thinking and the honest use of language.

As a movement, Christian humanism began in the 1300s among poets and writers in "the humanities," from which the movement first took its name. They were the very first to offer a distinctively modern critical engagement with the Bible and with the evolution of Christian belief in classical antiquity. They were also the first thinkers in the West to begin to recognize the extraordinary power of *cultural context*. Over time, as their thinking rippled through the culture, it evoked what we now call "the Renaissance."

PREFACE

Eight centuries later, however, "humanism" has acquired a much broader frame of reference. It is no longer a specifically Christian intellectual tradition. Today there are secular humanists, Buddhist humanists, Hindu humanists, Jewish humanists (secular and religious both), Muslim humanists, and so forth. We share a pragmatic, morally sensitive commitment to critical thinking and to the common good, with a strong emphasis on clear language and accurate information. "Humanism" has of course been vilified on the Far Right as rabidly antireligious if not downright demonic. But humanism properly defined has never been opposed to *religion*. Many of the most eminent Christian-humanist scholars have been clergy. Christian humanism is opposed to the *abuse* of religion. It is particularly opposed to the willful distortion of ancient religious texts and traditions by those who have contemporary political and economic ambitions.

My second useful concept is *moral imagination*. Imagination properly defined is the human cognitive ability to cope with paradox, to recognize patterns, and to think symbolically about a complex, polyvalent, dynamic reality. That's what Einstein was talking about when he said that imagination is more important than knowledge. The specifically *moral* imagination is this cognitive ability focused upon ethical questions.

And so each book in this series focuses upon a moral failure of hard-Right "Christianism." In addition to being judgmental, it's anti-gay. It's anti-science. It's verbally violent and implicitly theocratic, harkening back to crusades and inquisitions. It's literal minded and absolutist. Its agenda is flatly opposed to what the historical Jesus of Nazareth had to say for himself. And it celebrates a controlling God who is both crazy violent and vindictive. The first chapter of each volume is available as a free download on my website, CatherineM-Wallace.com.

In each of these books, on an issue-by-issue basis, I offer for your consideration some bit of wisdom provided by the specifically *Christian* moral imagination. That's not a covert "come to Jesus" plea. It's a plea to recognize that an immense cultural heritage is at risk no less decisively than statues of the Buddha blown up by the Taliban. I will offer insight that you don't have to become Christian to admire, just as you don't have to become Buddhist to admire Buddhist insight. To paraphrase the Dalai Lama, the point here is not becoming Christian. The point is to become wise.

And part of the wisdom we desperately need right now is the wisdom to deny Christian religious legitimacy to hatemongering distortions of a great tradition.

Acknowledgements

In the decade I spent working on this book and others like it, I was repeatedly cheered on by generous audiences and critical readers. I owe a lot to these good people and to the local congregations or civic organizations that invited me to speak. These audiences read or listened patiently as I struggled to get my thinking in order and my sources under control. They patiently endured academic digressions that I later deleted. They convinced me that the world is full of open-minded, compassionate, morally sensitive people who delight in the quirky facts of cultural history.

Above all, they influenced my writing in quite remarkable ways. They insisted that stories are crucial and so I should tell more of them. One evening I worried aloud that the storytelling was distracting. Didn't it disrupt the flow of my argument?

"Look," one woman insisted sharply, "That's how I know it's an important point. You stop and tell a story." Everyone else nodded. Well, okay then. Stories. The more stories I told, the more often audiences told me that the stories were crucial.

Audiences also gave me permission to restate classical issues in philosophy or theology using very down-to-earth language. During discussion after my presentation, I'd reframe some complicated issue with an "it's like this" analogy. *Say that,* people would insist. *Just say that. Why didn't you just say that in the first place?* Let me tell you why: I was haunted by the Ghost of Professors Past, that's why. In time I banished that ghost (well, mostly). But I could never have done so without their flat-out and repeated insistence that they wanted to hear this more immediate, more vulnerable voice.

ACKNOWLEDGEMENTS

And that's not all. They convinced me I had to keep going. Their raw anger and bitter frustration kept me at my desk. I realized that there are a lot of us—Christian humanists and secular humanists alike—who sharply oppose the hard-Right, highly politicized misappropriation of Christianity. Lots of people are eager for the backstory and the alternatives that I have to offer. They don't have the time to read all the stuff that I've read, and furthermore they don't have the scholarly background some of my sources presuppose. But they are just as curious and just as passionate as I am. They were as happy to find me as I've been to find a clever app. We need one another's skills.

In my audiences were Christians who are angry that the Christian "brand" has lost all connection to Jesus of Nazareth. They want their religion back. They want their God back. They are seriously pissed that "Christian" has come to mean "ignorant bigot," even though they understand that perception. They want a better public identity than "I'm not *that* kind of Christian." *Christian humanism* names the heritage and the values they cherish.

In my audiences were secular humanists. Some are outraged by encounters with "church people." Their stories haunt me. Some are outraged by the transparently anti-intellectual and theocratic ambitions of the radical Religious Right. They are offended by claims that this is a "Christian" nation and so one narrow version of Christianity should be allowed to usurp the law of the land and the democratic process. Many secular humanists are of course ex-Christians. Some reject that rigid, judgmental, hard-Right religiosity, which was the only version of Christianity available to them. Others have drifted away from dysfunctional congregations or from a faith that felt self-absorbed, irrelevantly dogmatic, and remote from the actual moral issues confounding daily life. Still others have tough and honest questions about the intellectual consistency of Christian beliefs or about Christian complicity in wrongdoing of one kind or another. Clergy or Sunday school teachers dodged these questions. That was that, as far as they were concerned. I have to respect anyone who takes religion seriously enough to reject incoherent versions.

And so I was honored by their willingness to listen to me. I was honored that they realized I'm not trying to convert anybody.

ACKNOWLEDGEMENTS

They trusted me on that point. And they pushed hard, asking terrific questions and holding their ground when I pushed back. That process helped me clarify my thinking. It helped me understand my primary audience, which *is* secular humanists.

Some in my audiences belonged to other faith traditions. These people are often quite eloquent about what they have found and why they value it. That too was invaluable. They helped me to find a conceptual language sufficiently open to communicate broadly.

Late in the process, I discovered major public affirmation of conversations like the ones I'd been having for ten years. In April 2014, the Brookings Institute issued a report, *Faith in Equality*, calling on Christian political progressives like me to reach out both to secular political progressives and to politically progressive religious conservatives for whom "Christianity" still has a clear theological connection to what Jesus actually taught about inclusivity, the image of God in everyone, and social justice as delineated by the great Jewish prophets. I take this report as evidence that the tide is turning nationally in opposition to hard-Right reactionaries in the Christian tradition.

I'm delighted to be part of that. I'm even more delighted to feel that I am speaking both to and for a solid core of ordinary, moderate, religiously tolerant Americans.

Grace and peace be with us all.

1

Confronting Fundamentalism: It's Judgmental

Nobody likes a bully. And yet bullying permeates our society. It's everywhere—from playgrounds to cable channels to online comments posted anonymously. Among the young it appears in crude and childish ways; among adults, it sometimes takes the more sophisticated form we call "judgmentalism." Judgmentalism is the casual willingness to condemn, ridicule, and deride others. Despite differences in style between bullies and the judgmental, it's all the same behavior. And it's everywhere.

In its Christian forms, judgmentalism invokes the transcendent as an ally by portraying God as a condemning judge. It usurps for its own purposes the symbolic and cultural capital of Christian religious tradition. That misappropriation, unopposed, will obliterate a major human heritage: the Christian understanding that authentic moral judgment is rooted in conscience as a creative process. "Morality" is not a set of rules to obey. Morality is an art. Arts cannot be reduced to rules and absolutes that can be weaponized to attack others.

In order to confront and oppose religious judgmentalism, we must first understand the core dynamics of bullying. That core dynamic turned out to be far more complex than I realized at first. Here's the issue: bullying in effect attempts to create a community—a set of social bonds—based on hostility and exclusion. This community sustains its status as the insiders or the acceptable ones through the ridicule, derision, exclusion, and condemnation of individuals identified as the outcast or the unacceptable. That community-building function accounts for why bullied children are such incessant targets for their classmates. The peer group coalesced around the most outspoken bullies depends upon these targets for its own unity and self-affirmation. *We know we are cool because we are not like her.*

That community-building dynamic is visible in the history of word "bully." The English word is derived from a Dutch word meaning "sweetheart" or "lover," probably from a Middle Dutch word for "brother." Originally (in the 1500s) it meant "a fine fellow." But over the course of the 1600s, the word began to be used sarcastically. As a result, its meaning gradually shifted to what we now mean by "bully." Bullies use derision of others as a way to claim their own value, their cherished place in a given social cohort, and the valuable exclusivity of the cohort itself. *We are "brothers." And you, buddy, are not one of us. We don't want you on our team.*

Judgmentalism is this ordinary schoolyard bullying directed against groups rather than individuals. Its targets can be distant and even unknown on a personal basis, although of course individual members of a targeted group might be attacked if opportunity presents itself. Judgmentalism serves the same social purposes that bullying serves: it affirms the value or status of the judgmental person, and it seeks to create or to sustain a group by creating outcasts. Judgmentalism creates and repeatedly reaffirms the vital division between us and them, between the acceptable in-group and the unacceptable out-group.

Sophisticated Christian moral judgment, on the other hand, seeks to create or to sustain a group through hospitality, not hostility. ("Hospitality" and "hostility" share a common linguistic stem, a word meaning "stranger." Outsiders—those who are unfamiliar in some regard—can be welcomed as guests or rejected as threats.) Hospitality is inclusive, not exclusive. Its core behaviors are not ridicule, derision, and condemnation, but rather empathy (I care how you feel), respect (I value who you are), and deference (you have perspectives or gifts from which I can learn). The hospitable welcome diversity as a source of strength and skill. In folklore, for instance, the stranger commonly has some strange but vitally important gift to offer.[1] The hostile see differences as threats.

In short, hospitality and hostility are two different systems of social organization. They are two different politics. Hostile groups divide the world between us and them, who are to be attacked and excluded. Hospitable groups recognize that we are all in this together, and so we must devise ways to collaborate. Hospitable groups rely upon rules for collaboration, which are, first, the principles of hospitality, and second, the principles of classic, evidence-based analysis and persuasion. Hostile groups, on the other hand, try to win their way by belittling and berating others rather than by arguing the issues in accord with public standards of intellectual validity and globally recognized moral norms.

Hospitality, especially the radical hospitality proclaimed by Jesus of Nazareth, is part of the moral heritage at risk.

The Power of Bullies

I think we all recognize the social power exerted by bullies. We all react to derision, whether it's directed at us or whether we are merely bystanders. We feel the power of the implicit politics set into action by the bully. The power of the bully is the power of shame, one of the most potent social emotions that we experience.

The bullies and the judgmental both seek to shame. They seek to exclude people by shaming them, which is to say declaring that this person or these people are in some key regard inadequate, unworthy, not "enough" of something or other. When it's done shrewdly, when it's done skillfully and by those with highly polished PR skills and high-wattage media outlets, it's powerfully persuasive for many people. People go along rather than risk becoming the target of such vitriolic attack.

Religionized shaming is a fascinating, complicated issue in America because we think we are not a shame-based culture at

---

1. Lewis Hyde discusses that folklore in his famous little book, *The Gift*.

all. Shame (or "face" and the loss of "face") is an issue in China, we think, or in the Middle East, but not here! Certainly not! Ah, but it is an issue—and in culturally quite specific terms. Shame is an even more powerful issue among us because we don't commonly recognize what these terms are.

Bullying and judgmentalism succeed—they are politically powerful strategies in our society—because we lack a clear understanding of moral judgment. I'm not saying we don't have good moral judgment. I think most of us do. I'm saying we don't have a clear understanding of what our good moral judgment entails, or how it works, or why it's reliable, and above all what its appropriate limits are. As a result, we live with a certain level of moral uncertainty.

In the absence of this clear understanding of moral judgment, people committed to fact-based analysis sometimes fail to use the language of moral judgment in politically effective ways. Progressives are apt to show up with tables and graphs and complicated analyses; the hard Right, meanwhile, thunders about right and wrong, claiming the moral high ground. It is as if facts and morality have no relationship to one another at all. This situation, familiar to all of us, attests painfully to the destruction of a major cultural heritage. I want to reclaim that heritage, or to begin the reclaiming, by sketching its outline in plain, accessible terms.

Religious judgmentalism obscures an ancient moral heritage of hard-won wisdom about what's required of us if we are to live together in peace as a human community. From the time of Homer's epic account of the Trojan War, after all, it has been recognized that honest critical analysis and debate is the great alternative to bloodshed and battle. But Christian fundamentalist judgmentalism obscures these ancient methods and frameworks for morally sensitive, nuanced, collaborative critical thinking and problem solving. Reclaiming that wisdom is the best way (and perhaps the only way) to discredit judgmental religionized bullying within Christian tradition. Other Christians must stand up and speak up. Christian humanists and humanists in other traditions need to affirm the humane values and intellectual commitments that we share despite important differences in our religious and philosophical allegiances.

CONFRONTING FUNDAMENTALISM: IT'S JUDGMENTAL

Overview

In chapter 2 I'll tell a story—a whole series of stories, in fact—about moments in my own life when I came face to face with my own uncertainties about moral judgment. I could see things happening in the world around me that I felt were *wrong*. People sometimes died as the result of what somebody saw as morally justified behavior. These experiences motivated the reading and the questioning behind the argument I'll share later on: how does anybody know what's right and what's wrong?

In chapter 3, I'll sketch my understanding of how shame, bullying, and moral uncertainty function in American culture. In our diverse, often anonymous, sharply competitive society, we face a continual cultural pressure to "prove ourselves," to "measure up," to "compete successfully." That's a setup for feeling chronically inadequate, because it's never clear to whom exactly we are trying to prove ourselves. The necessary proof never arrives in our psychosocial inbox, suitable for framing. In its absence, we struggle with *shame*.

In an American context, it's acutely shameful to struggle with shame at all. We are not supposed to have self-doubts. We are all supposed to be rugged individualists, fully self-realized and confidently self-affirming (plus cool, successful, and of course buff—don't forget buff). Our shame and denial around the very fact of shame helps to explain why religionized shaming is a culturally powerful political tool.

In chapter 4, I'll stop and tell a story that tries to create a bridge between Christian theological concepts and what all of us already know about our own struggles with self-doubt or self-criticism. Here's the story in preview: I was a stubborn kid. I was mediocre academically and yet taunted endlessly for being a "brain." All of that made me more stubborn and more resistant to everyone around me, kids and adults alike, who disapproved of me so unanimously. And one day I realized something: I also disagreed with the teaching that all of us are "sinners." That's not how God saw me.

In chapter 5, I'll take a sharp look at religionized judgmentalism in the Christian tradition. Christianity as many people have encountered it seems to insist that we *ought* to be ashamed of ourselves. In

God's eyes, supposedly, we are all personally inadequate. We are all moral failures. That sweeping condemnation goes back, supposedly, to the "original sin" of Adam and Eve in the garden of Eden. And so, in chapter 5 I'll offer a very different interpretation of that story, an interpretation based on Robin Stockitt's biblical scholarship in *Restoring the Shamed: Toward a Theology of Shame* (2012).

From this interpretation I'll offer a major conclusion: Christianity properly understood offers a potent antidote to abusive religionized shaming. This antidote is radical hospitality. Radical hospitality is the genuine heritage of the historical Jesus of Nazareth. Whether or not Jesus was divine—a question I'll defer to *The Confrontational Wit of Jesus* [forthcoming], chapter 5—he had dramatic things to say about inclusive community. And he reserved his sharpest criticism for those who used religious tradition to condemn and exclude others.

In chapter 6, I ask an obvious question. If Christianity is what I say Christianity is, then where did this religious judgmentalism come from? There's quite a backstory here. Religious judgmentalism in its contemporary form arose as a by-product of the radical religious literalism which appeared in the 1870s and 1880s. This literalism explicitly rejected scholarship both in the sciences and in the humanities. It was sweepingly, explicitly anti-intellectual.

But more centrally, and far more dangerously, Christian judgmentalism arose as an aspect of Christian theocracy in the West: over centuries, theocracy had come to portray God as a violent, vindictive judge. A violent, vindictive God is of course politically useful: he provides cosmic cover for political violence. But by the same measure, such theology is itself dangerous. It contributed in no small measure to Europe's devastating Wars of Religion (1524–1660), discussed in detail in *Confronting Religious Absolutism* [forthcoming], chapter 4.

In chapter 7 I'll explain how this heritage generates a problem that we still have trouble solving. We have trouble even seeing it clearly. Here's the problem: Can we have good moral judgment without being *judgmental*? Can we have a coherent morality without becoming *moralistic*?

CONFRONTING FUNDAMENTALISM: IT'S JUDGMENTAL

It seems to me that the moral nihilism of the hard Left is just as incoherent as the judgmental moralism of the hard Right. On the hard Left, "tolerance" is the greatest good. Should we then tolerate the intolerant? If not, are we contradicting ourselves? If morality is all "personal opinion," then the religiously judgmental have a right to their opinions, don't they? Who are we to complain about how broadly they condemn gay people, single mothers, immigrants, the unemployed or unemployable, people surviving on Social Security benefits, and even graduate students who need insurance coverage for contraceptives? How can we oppose their vilification of climate scientists, biologists, religious minorities, immigrants, refugees, and advocates for the underpaid and unemployed? Progressives and moderates need to reclaim the language of moral judgment—the language of right and wrong—but without giving in to an equal and opposite judgmentalism.

Is that possible? Can we talk about morality without being moralistic? Can we debate issues of difficult moral judgment (like climate policy or immigration reform) without being judgmental? What's the role of fact or data in such discussions?

In chapters 8 and 9, I offer an exceedingly brief survey of European intellectual efforts, in the wake of the great religious wars, to answer such questions. Enlightenment thinkers sought an objective, intellectually rigorous basis for moral judgment. These efforts have been called "the great Enlightenment project." It failed. We should be glad it failed. If it had succeeded in its own rigorously intellectual terms, then we would have landed in the philosophical equivalent of theocracy: totalitarianism. In the twentieth century, secular totalitarianism proved even more deadly than theocracy. But philosophers in the 1700s had some brilliant insights nonetheless. You will undoubtedly recognize some of these ideas even if you've never read a single word of eighteenth-century philosophy.

In chapters 10–12, I lay out a Christian humanist basis for moral judgment: conscience is a creative process, which is to say moral judgment is an art. Moral judgment is a set of skillful practices, not obedience to a rigid ideology or a strict philosophical construction. Here's how that will go:

CONFRONTING RELIGIOUS JUDGMENTALISM

- In chapter 10, I acknowledge that my position is rooted in a biblical assumption: human nature is inherently prosocial. We are inherently good and we are inherently attracted to the good available to us within whatever choices we face in life. But these are not narrowly doctrinal or dogmatic claims. They are widely shared among other religions. There's also excellent scientific evidence that we are innately prosocial. As starting points go, mine is conceptually as inclusive as any starting point can be without backing into unworkable philosophical absolutes. I do my best here to pull together valuable insights gleaned from philosophy and from our own common sense.

- In chapter 11, I admit that my position is also "heretical" in the eyes of Christians who define God as the Cosmic Condemning Judge, not the cosmic source of all compassion and kindness. I offer a bit of backstory explaining certain "security liabilities" in Christian theological tradition, liabilities into which the Religious Right has "hacked" for political purposes.

- In chapter 12, I lay out in detail how conscience functions as a creative process which synthesizes globally recognized moral norms (*Thou shalt not kill*, etc.) with the messy particulars of our own immediate situation. The result is a reasoned moral autonomy that is nonetheless distinct from both fundamentalist judgmentalism and anything-goes nihilism. (If you want to read chapter 12 first, that's fine. I worked hard to make sure that would work because I read that way myself sometimes, jumping around in a book before settling down for a cover-to-cover feast.)

- In chapter 13, I conclude with a reconsideration of my flame-out with my teenage son, the story I begin with in chapter 3. Like all good sons everywhere, that kid knew his mother's hot buttons. . . .

2

1998, 1968, 1970: *Just an Opinion*

1998: As the Light Turned Green

We were waiting to turn left at the light when my son cut loose.

"At lunch yesterday," he said, "Ibrahim wouldn't eat lunch. It's Ramadan. Jacob won't eat pork: he's Jewish. Joe won't eat meat on Fridays because he's Catholic. Ram never eats meat—he's Hindu. It's all opinion. All this right-and-wrong stuff is just opinion!"

By this point I'd pulled into the drop-off driveway. He was halfway out of the car before I found my voice. I took a deep breath and spoke without thinking.

"I think Jake would say eating pork is only one kind of wrong. The Holocaust was another kind." I spoke much more sharply than I intended.

My son's head snapped up.

We lived in Skokie. Plenty of his friends' grandparents had blue numbers tattooed on their forearms.

Good Lord, had I just played the Holocaust card against my own son?

He had it coming, muttered a voice within me.

That's bullshit and you know it's bullshit, another voice replied. *What, you think he doesn't know the difference between kosher and murder?*

My son opened the sliding door to get some project from the back seat. I twisted around, fighting against the seat belt, trying to see his face.

"Good luck with your presentation," I said blandly, as if nothing had just happened—hoping nothing had just happened, hoping he wasn't listening. Teenagers are often not listening, after all. Yes? Isn't that true? Wasn't he tuning me out so completely he hadn't heard?

He half glanced in my direction, avoiding eye contact, his face inscrutable.

"Yep. Thanks for the ride." He spoke as neutrally as I had.

I sat there a minute, watching him walk away, until the car behind me honked.

"It's *all* opinion." That had annoyed me far more than his intelligent skepticism about rules for fasting. Did he know that? Maybe not. Maybe I'd blown it. I'd fallen hard for that classic adolescent trick, the zinger tossed off when there's no time to think. I drove home repenting my short temper and quick tongue.

Really, kid, don't pull stunts like that so early in the morning. I'm a recovering academic. Cut me some slack once in a while.

My son is now in his mid-thirties. So I asked him. He remembers. As clearly as I do.

1968: The Pope's Opinion

I was eighteen years old myself—newly graduated from high school—when my own mother did something no less memorable.

In that summer, the summer of 1968, Pope Paul VI issued his famous encyclical *Humanae Vitae*. In that papal letter to Catholics everywhere, the pope repeated the Roman Catholic ban on birth control. In doing so, he overruled the consensus of his own theological commission, whose findings in favor of birth control had already been announced to the press.

In my junior year (1966–1967), the nun teaching my religion class clearly knew what this panel of experts was reporting to the pope. Sister Mary Fidelia lectured us carefully on the advantages and disadvantages and failure rates of every possible form of birth control—necessary information for after we were married, of course. We were not allowed to take notes, which ensured that we paid particularly close attention as Sister drew various IUDs on the blackboard, insisted that diaphragms had to be professionally fitted, and explained how birth control pills worked. (Birth control pills had been approved by the FDA in 1961, although a federal right to contraception for married couples was not established until June of 1965, the end of my freshman year of high school.) Sister also explained that we needed permission from a priest to use birth control, but that requirement was framed by her much more vehement assertion that it's morally wrong to conceive more children than one can nurture emotionally and provide for materially. And, needless to say, it is immoral to force a woman to endure more pregnancies than her own health allows. The nuns might not have known about the physical demands of pregnancy, but they spent their days with children who were one of eight or ten or twelve children in their families. They knew. Sister Mary Fidelia spoke to us with all the authority nuns are famous for projecting.

She never said what we should do if a priest refused permission. But the answer seemed perfectly clear, at least to me. Consult a different priest. Find one who would listen. My mother and her friends talked about that openly: some priests were idiots, but some were not. Priests, like nuns, were as various as any other group of human beings. *Find a good one.*

But on that summer day in 1968, Catholics learned that priests who deferred obediently to the pope's authority would henceforth always deny permission to use birth control. I still remember the audible gasp in the church when the pastor read to the congregation a short summary of the pope's ruling, a summary that must have been mailed out to parishes from the archbishop's office downtown. He held it out at arm's length, flapping it in the air, making it clear that the cardinal had said that the pope had said and that he had been told to tell us. And so he did, reading aloud in a stiff and stilted way, holding the pages up as he did so.

After mass my mother sternly ordered, "Come with me." Mom was a tiny, outgoing, fiercely determined woman. I followed in her wake like a tall, unsteady sailboat. We cut through the small side door to the left of the altar and hurried out to the wide paved alley between the church and the parish grade school.

There we joined a growing knot of her friends, all of them adamant and angry. I listened, wide-eyed, to the eruption. One line echoed over and over again: "No daughter of mine . . . No daughter of mine . . ." We their almost innumerable daughters were not to have innumerable pregnancies. The pope was wrong. The cardinal was a toady. The pastor was a wimp. I listened intently as these angry women insisted that they would decide about birth control for themselves—the pope be damned. I'd heard plenty of complaints about the church over the years, but those complaints were always tempered and framed by an underlying deference, an underlying deep respect for the church as *the church*. I'd never heard anything like this.

And I'd never seen such defiant women. This was not feminist outrage. When *The Feminine Mystique* had been published five years earlier, my mother had dismissed Betty Friedan as a bored rich woman—a woman who had been to college, for heaven's sake, a woman who didn't know how good she had it. My mother and her friends were not complaining that they were oppressed by a sexist institution. They were making a much darker accusation.

They were saying that the pope was morally wrong. They held his authority up against their own experience as the mothers of families—sometimes very large families—and they claimed an authority that trumped his. Their own experience, their knowledge of one another's lives, their maternal wisdom about what children need—all of that added up to something weightier than the power of the Vicar of Christ on Earth. He was *wrong*.

I suspect that if they had felt alone or isolated, none of them would have defied church authority like this. But together they were unstoppable. This was something deeper than garden-variety 1960s bra-burning feminist outrage. This was what African-American theologians would later call "womanist."

At the time, I didn't know what to make of what I was seeing. I had never heard adults so openly and profoundly challenge the church. Why had Mom told me to come with her? She might have told me to walk home alone, that she had something to do. That would have been commonplace. Why was I here? No other woman had any of her daughters with her. What was going on here?

Something much more than I understood, that's for sure.

A World Unraveling

When I look back now, I can laugh at my own consternation: Mom always did worry about my reticence. I was as shy as she was outgoing: we baffled one another incessantly. No doubt on this occasion she felt I needed a good dose of uppity womanhood—and perhaps some clarity about birth control before I left for college. No doubt she was right on both points.

And yet, at the time there was nothing comic about that scene. At the time, in the summer of 1968, there was very little to laugh about.

As I looked out at the world I was poised to inherit, I was increasingly uncertain. In January the Viet Cong Tet Offensive had begun to turn the tide of that deeply controversial war: the eventual American defeat began to loom on the horizon. In April I had stood on an expressway overpass—the closest thing Chicago has to a hill. I looked east, toward Lake Michigan and inner city neighborhoods, watching black smoke billowing from riots after the murder of Martin Luther King Jr. In June, just days before my high school graduation, Robert Kennedy had also been murdered.

The nuns had made the class valedictorian rewrite her valedictory address: I remember seeing Claire standing in tears in the hallway, surrounded by the other top honors students. That was not my group; I stood on the edges only long enough to figure out what was wrong. Girls were arguing that graduation was *our* day and why should *their* problems intrude?

Their problems? If we were adults now, which was what everyone was saying, surely these were now *our* problems as well. What, did these girls intend to remain sheltered daughters? I never did understand that group.

As I packed for college in August, I listened on my bedroom radio to news reports of the police riots at the Democratic National Convention downtown. I wanted to go to Grant Park to look around for myself. My father—resting on the sofa, recuperating from surgery—sat up abruptly, flatly forbidding me to set foot outside the house. I deferred unquestioningly to his authority. I deferred almost gratefully, perhaps: maybe it wasn't so bad to be a sheltered daughter, at least for a few more weeks. I was leaving soon enough.

In the years since then I've heard too many stories from friends who had been in Grant Park at the time. Chicago police cordoned off peaceful anti-war protestors, then attacked with phalanx after phalanx of helmeted, club-wielding cops. Cops chased fleeing kids into locked doorways and blind alleys, shattering their skulls, leaving them unconscious in pools of blood. Some journalists got some pictures and escaped with their cameras unsmashed, but many were severely injured. Their reporting was both courageous and historically significant, and I remember it each time I hear NPR recordings from journalists on the ground amidst peaceful protests similarly set upon by government forces.

My Invisible Box

I left for college that August with a single suitcase in my left hand. It was green, a graduation gift from my godmother. Tucked under my right arm was my prize possession, a graduation gift from my parents: a small portable typewriter in its own blue zippered case. Trailing after me, as if under its own power, was an invisible carton bulging with one question, and one question only: *how do you know?*

"How do you know?" has many specific forms. How do you know what's right and what's wrong, what's just and what's unjust? How do you know how to live your own life amidst such huge and unanswerable questions? Can anyone be trusted? Can the validity of any truth claim be established at all? *How do you know?*

Like every other first-wave Boomer, I came of age in a world that seemed to be unraveling. Everywhere I looked, a single sharp-edged question was slowly but steadily slicing away at the fabric of 1950s certainty: *How do you know?* In 1968, *How do you know?* did not feel like an abstractly philosophical issue. In my world, it had an overwhelming immediacy. Disputes about how to define morality translated swiftly to smoke in the skies and blood on the street. Disputes about the true and the false translated into horrific film clips of Buddhist monks burning themselves alive to protest the war, or that famous photograph of a naked girl running away from her napalm-bombed village, where her parents and siblings might have been burned alive. Our moral positions had mortally dangerous consequences like these.

Figuring out where I stood and why felt far more important than French 101 or freshman composition.

1970: Kent State

Just two years later—on Monday, May 4, 1970—National Guardsmen fired on peaceful, unarmed Kent State students protesting the American bombing of Cambodia. My brother, who had signed up for the Air Force rather than be drafted into the Army, was one of those pilots. We didn't know that at the time, of course: he was simply one of many pilots in the war. One of the dead students was a woman who had been walking past that protest en route to her one o'clock history course. I too had a one o'clock history course that term. She was a sophomore. I was a sophomore. She was an honors student. So was I. Had I gone to Kent State, I'm sure I would have known her. *I might have been her.*

She bled to death on the sidewalk. I did not. I stared at her picture on the news, that famous picture of one woman looking up and screaming over the body of another woman lying there in a puddle of her own blood. That body on the sidewalk might have been me. For the last forty-some years I have remembered her at every milestone of my own life: graduation, marriage, children, grandchildren, every experience I got to have that she didn't get to have because she bled to death on a sidewalk. But I didn't: I survived. I have prayed for her family and her friends, who have no doubt missed her presence at each of these moments in their own lives. She is for me an icon of a past that remains stunningly present.

On that night in May, my mother was on the phone with my large extended family assuring everyone that I was safe at home. When my parents' friends could not get through on the phone, they flocked to our house in person. When I answered the door, I was embraced in hugs I have never forgotten. All of these familiar faces were in tears. Even the dads were in tears, their rough-shaved faces wet against mine. Our was one of the rare households where kids had gone *away* to college. Ordinarily, if kids went to college at all, it was as a commuter to Loyola or DePaul or the Chicago branch of the University of Illinois. All these parents knew where their kids were. I was the one who came to mind when the news about Kent State flashed on the radio. There were protests on campuses nationwide: who knew how many other kids would be dead by morning if the government continued shooting at unarmed protestors.

When the living room filled, latecomers flowed into the dining room, all of them arguing about a government gone mad. To one side of the dining room was a hallway, and from that hallway rose a flight of stairs leading to our bedrooms. I sat on those stairs hugging my knees, listening not to the voices but to the tone of voice, to the panic and the anger.

And then I left by the side door. I went out to have pizza with a guy who sat behind me in that one o'clock history course. I had no idea who he was, but he'd called when he first heard the news about Kent State. He invited me to join him for deep-dish pizza at Uno's. It wasn't called "Chicago-style" pizza then. It was just Uno's. Ordinarily I would not have agreed to a date with a guy I didn't know, but amidst the news of the day I yearned for some contact, any contact, with the campus world I'd left behind. Long-distance phone calls were outrageously expensive, and ours was a working-class household: it never occurred to me to phone anyone.

On a Monday night, Uno's was empty. It was not yet a tourist destination. We sat quietly at a graffiti-scarred black table, eating our pizza, struggling to make sense of a world that had come apart at the seams. We drove home through empty streets in a dark and silent city, past neighborhoods still boarded up after the riots following the murder of Dr. King two years earlier. I had stayed out long after my curfew.

I opened the side door as quietly as I could. Our elderly collie lumbered up the basement steps from her plaid bed, greeting me groggily. My parents did not waken, or if they wakened they did not say anything. Ordinarily they would have. And in the morning, they did not reprimand me.

I've never been back to Uno's, a Chicago landmark just blocks from our apartment. Its scarred black tables still haunt my nightmares. Right and wrong is just an opinion? Whose opinion? And who will die as a result?

How do you know? It's a question gouged deep in the Western soul.

3

Shame and the American Character

Moralistic judgmentalism in an American setting is both politically powerful and culturally toxic because it exploits deep-seated psychological liabilities in the American character. Here's the liability: the highly competitive American culture challenges each of us to construct our core identity in isolation both from the cultural past and from a small, loyal, affirming community within which we work and live.

And then, furthermore, we need to prove the value of what we have constructed. Prove to whom? Prove to whomever. That's part of the problem: to whom are we struggling to prove ourselves? That's never entirely clear. And so there's never an entirely clear answer. There's never a proof that concludes with a satisfying QED, *quod erat demonstrandum*. Neither does the bluebird of happiness land on our shoulders announcing, *You have made it, babe. Yessiree, you have once and for all time and beyond all doubt ARRIVED.*

As a result, it's easy to feel lost in a fog of insanely perfectionist standards: I'm a failure if I'm not as successful as the most successful, as talented as the most talented, as socially adept as the most adept, as buff and gorgeous as the models in advertisements. To be flawed in any way, to be limited in any way, is somehow shameful. But to be human is to be flawed and limited. There's no escaping that. And so, if we reject our own humanity, of course we doom ourselves to live in fear of rejection by others.

In Christian humanist terms, we struggle with such anxieties because we fail to understand that despite our limitations we are good people. We are made in the image of God, in whose eyes we are lovely. In God's eyes, so to speak, we are lovely not *despite* our humanity but *because of* our humanity. Real beauty is far more complex than perfection. Perfection is simple and static and in control. Beauty is alive and complex; beauty is dynamic and engaging just as love is dynamic and engaging. In God's eyes we are *beautiful*, not *perfect*. We are made by love for love, not by static perfection for static perfection.

Our perfectionist, self-critical, competitive anxieties are all versions or varieties of *shame*. Shame is a pervasive and in some ways invisible problem. Shame is moral judgment gone awry. Shame is judgmental ridicule and derision directed against ourselves rather than against those we reject as "outsiders." When we give way to this inward judgmentalism, we define ourselves as "outsiders." We make ourselves feel like misfits. We make ourselves feel that we don't "belong" in some invisible way that is available to everyone else. Don't get me wrong: those feelings are real, and they're powerful, and they may not seem self-generated. But they are. That's the power of shame. Understanding the power of shame is vitally important to confronting the cultural influence of hard-Right, highly politicized religious judgmentalism.

Brené Brown, who has spent her career researching shame and shame resilience, defines shame as "the intensely painful feeling or experience of believing we are flawed and therefore unworthy of acceptance or belonging."[1] Robin Stockitt, the biblical scholar I mentioned earlier, defined "shame" as "The fear . . . that if one's true nature is transparently clear for all to see, then one runs the risk of being scorned, humiliated, and ultimately rejected."[2] Buddhist teacher and clinical psychologist Tara Brach opens her book *Radical Acceptance* (2003) with a series of metaphors for what shame feels

1. Brown, *I Thought It Was Just Me*, chapter 1.
2. Stockitt, *Restoring the Shamed*, 68.

like. Those metaphors define "shame" as cogently as anything I've ever read:

> For years I've had a recurring dream in which I am caught in a futile struggle to get somewhere. Sometimes I'm running up a hill; sometimes I am climbing over boulders or swimming against a current. Often a loved one is in trouble or something bad is about to happen. My mind is speeding frantically, but my body feels heavy and exhausted; I move as if through molasses. I know I should be able to handle the problem, but no matter how hard I try, I can't get where I need to go. Completely alone and shadowed by the fear of failure, I am trapped in my dilemma. Nothing else in the world exists but that.
>
> This dream captures the essence of the trance of unworthiness . . . We are living in a waking dream that completely defines and delimits our experience of life. The rest of the world is merely a backdrop as we struggle to get somewhere, to be a better person, to accomplish, to avoid making mistakes. . . . Inherent in the trance is the belief that no matter how hard we try, we always, in some ways, fall short. Feeling unworthy goes hand in hand with feeling separate from others, separate from life. If we are defective, how can we possibly belong? It's a vicious cycle: The more deficient we feel, the more separate and vulnerable we feel.[3]

Shame is far more than a negative self-image. Shame is self-condemnation projected out onto everyone around us, from whom as a result we feel painfully separated. Heaven help us, then, if among the people surrounding us there's a group claiming that God himself condemns and rejects us because we are unworthy.

As I see it, shame is derogatory judgmentalism directed inward, just as bullying is derogatory judgmentalism directed outward. And there's a deadly feedback loop between the two: our own fear of shame or being shamed can underlie our willingness to join someone in making derogatory comments about someone else. To counteract this deadly feedback loop between judgmentalism and

---

3. Brach, *Radical Acceptance*, 18.

our own fear of shame, we need to understand the peculiar cultural challenges we face as Americans. Shame is a pre-wired hot button in the American soul.

And Christianity as I understand it—Christianity in the centuries-old "humanist" tradition—can help us to dial back some of the voltage to that hot button. Or to shift metaphors, Christian humanism offers a precisely targeted antidote to the toxicity of fundamentalist judgmentalism.

Prove Yourself!

The first liability is the dark underside of the American Dream. Think of it, perhaps, as the American Nightmare.

If in America "you can be anything," if in America there are no obstacles to any of us rising as high as our talents can take us, then we are at fault if our lives turn out to be ordinary or, heaven help us, something of a struggle. Sociologists have been saying this for generations: "prove yourself" is corrosive.

And the question *Are you saved?* implicitly raises the threat of social disapproval to a metaphysical level, concentrating it with laser-like intensity: *What does God think of you? Do you measure up with God as well as I measure up with God?*

Spare me. *God damns nobody,* I want to say, *not even people who think that way about God.* And yet, given the theological assumption that God is the All-Critical Judge, then being "saved" can provide significant relief from all-American "prove yourself" pressures. In effect, Christians who think this way are recasting God as what Joss Whedon calls the Sky Bully—and then they are siding with God.

When our kids were in junior high, their walk to school took them past a small church. Week after week its billboard proclaimed a different version of "come to church or go to hell." Week after week the kids would ask me over dinner about that week's snippet of condescending hostility. In short order they understood that such threats are hollow—and furthermore that their mother could cut loose, under proper provocation, with an entertaining rant and perhaps sing a hymn verse with entirely new lyrics, composed on the spot. (Rewriting hymn lyrics was easier if I was having a beer with dinner. With three kids in junior high, I often felt that a beer with dinner was medically indicated.)

The people attending that church probably never realized that week after week their billboard proclaimed to the unchurched and the non-Christian, *God hates you, God hates you, God hates you.* They more likely saw it as something closer to "we have been spared the wrath of God and you can be too—so get in here before it's too late."

Christian humanism offers an antidote to such fears by insisting that God is not the Condemning Judge critically inspecting our every failure. We never have to prove ourselves to God. Major traditions within Christianity flatly insist that God has already made up God's mind about us (so to speak): God loves each of us beyond our wildest imagining and without regard to what we or anyone else thinks about our "deserving" or "not deserving." God already understands our deepest fears and self-unworthiness. God thinks—bottom line—that such self-condemnation and self-unworthiness are complete balderdash. We should stop beating ourselves up, because self-aversion fuels the abuse of others.

If we could recognize how God loves us, Christian humanist tradition teaches, then we might stop trying to prove ourselves to one another in ways that are both self-defeating and more than a little toxic. If we are not endlessly contending with self-aversion, it will also be easier to admit our mistakes and to make prompt amends when we do screw up. Which we do. And which we will be tempted to deny if we are forever fending off self-aversion and self-condemnation. If my only choice is between "despicable" and "perfect," then by golly I'll pretend to be perfect. I'll blame somebody else or flat-out ignore my own mistakes.

Authentic religion in any tradition, I'd insist, opposes and attempts to neutralize the inhumane and dysfunctional aspects of the surrounding culture. Christian fundamentalism in the highly politicized form that has emerged in America instead exploits these problems for its own purposes. Religionized shaming drapes ridicule and derision in religious rhetoric and (supposedly) religious authority. Because America is by far the most religiously observant among major industrialized nations, such strategies are culturally quite effective.

⁎

The cultural demand to "prove ourselves," to "make something" of our lives, is not the only all-American liability that the religiously judgmental exploit. Our sense of isolation has also been exploited. Let's take a look at that next.

Needing to Belong

Religious judgmentalism exploits a second major liability in the American character, one that's closely related to the "prove yourself" trap: we do not have a secure community that clearly mirrors our identity back to us. As Robert Bellah and his associates documented decades ago in *Habits of the Heart* (1985), European immigrants to America cast off the constraints of a traditional social-class structure. Migrating to the New World offered the opportunity to build new lives and, along with these new lives, new identities that were entirely self-constructed (or so the story goes).

In the nineteenth century, popular culture insisted, "Go West, young man, go West!" That internal migration provided yet another major cultural opportunity to reboot identity, this time freed from the increasingly "civilized" Eastern seaboard.

In the early twentieth century, it happened again. The industrializing of agriculture displaced millions of American farmworkers, whose manual labor was no longer needed. Small towns emptied out as these workers left, followed by the small businesses that they had supported. Millions of people thus exchanged the social constraints of small-town rural life for the anonymity of big cities. Many of them were happy to do so: small towns seemed increasingly small-minded amidst the rapid cultural change elicited by new technologies like telephones, telegraphs, radio, an extensive railway system, electrification, and of course the automobile. Cities meant freedom, especially for the young and for black people fleeing the Klu Klux Klan and rural versions of Jim Crow laws.

Breaking with the past and chopping off our own roots have come to be expected. But freedom comes at a cost. We feel rootless. In each of these migrations, what was gained in psychosocial freedom was lost in psychosocial security. In tightly scripted communities, identity was secure even if it was constrained. Individuals had a clear place. They knew they belonged, even if their assigned roles were a poor fit with their talents, interests, and needs.

As a result, Bellah and his colleagues explain, Americans today are much better at devising ways to reach goals than we are at figuring out what our goals ought to be in the first place. What should we seek in life? Why should we seek it? People have trouble identifying those ultimate goals, Bellah and his colleagues discovered. When their book was first published (1985), there was much discussion about this finding.

Because we are social animals, I suggest, our sense of well-being is intrinsically dependent upon others: our ultimate goal in life is to know that we belong. We need to know that we are seen, that we are valued, that we are securely included. In traditional language, we need to love and to know that we are loved in return. In a national culture so profoundly shaped by dislocation from community, however, that need can be largely invisible and perhaps itself somewhat shameful. Our need to belong is somewhat shameful because we are not supposed to need to belong: we are all supposed to be rugged individualists, invulnerable in our self-confidence, courageously independent of needing anyone. (In a culture defined as "each against all," we need simply to impress people, or prove ourselves to people, or compete successfully against people. We don't need to love and be loved. Supposedly.)

In today's anonymous, mobile, highly competitive society, it can be difficult to establish this necessary sense of secure social belonging. It's difficult because, although we exist in a vast network of relationships, all these other people are not, in fact, a *community*. That is, the people we know do not all know one another. We don't live all in the same neighborhood. We don't spend our entire lives, from childhood to old age, in the comprehensive face-to-face community that almost everyone had until almost yesterday, by which I mean just a few centuries ago. Such communities have almost entirely disappeared from industrialized economies, which require workers to be mobile (and perhaps also to travel 50 percent of the time).

For a biologically social animal, that's extraordinarily stressful. We live our entire lives in a more-or-less permanent state of physiological alarm: *Help! Help! I've lost my herd!* On bad days we can feel like one among millions on some vast featureless plain, no matter how many friends we have on Facebook.

Millennials get a lot of grief on this topic. They are derided for their adept use of social media. Worse yet, perhaps, they get along with their parents! Bellah and his colleagues are right that breaking with tradition is the all-American tradition: the past is implicitly confining (supposedly), and so we must break with it in order to become authentic and self-realized. But who epitomizes the past more than one's parents? In American culture, the self-realized are the rootless, belonging only to themselves. By that measure, the highly networked Millennials are baffling if not revolutionary.

Given the inherent loneliness of these American cultural trends and expectations, it is more than a little obnoxious when any group as sharply organized and well-funded as the Religious Right expends so much time, money, and media skill proclaiming that some of us are outcasts and some of us are enemies of all that is morally decent. Worse yet, they do so in the name of God and in the language of an ancient, culturally powerful religious tradition. For those directly targeted by such denunciations and hate-mongering, that's not just missing our herd. That's feeling surrounded by predators. It's explicitly antisocial in ways that good people resent even when we ourselves are not singled out for condemnation (although in the end we too will be damned for our refusal to support such condemnation and exclusion).

Religious judgmentalism in Christian guise is doubly peculiar, theologically speaking, because classic Christian humanist theology so broadly and unequivocally insists that all of humanity is one. There exists a unity among all human beings that transcends all differences in race, creed, color, religion, language, ethnicity, gender, ability or disability, and so forth. We are all, equally, the beloved children of God. We belong to one another as intimately as if we were one small hunter-gatherer clan. We are morally responsible for one another's well-being. In fact, we are one with the planet and all that is on it and within it.

And not only that: as a Christian I am specifically enjoined to reach out to the stranger, to the immigrant, to the refugee, to the outcast, and to those regarded as "different" in any way at all. I am supposed to help such people to feel welcome and safe. I am supposed to build up safe and welcoming community, not tear it down. That teaching goes back to the very beginning of Christian tradition: it is far older than Christian humanism, which as a scholarly tradition goes back only to the 1300s. Welcoming the stranger, the immigrant, and the refugee is an aspect of Christian tradition that the humanists did not have to recover because it had never been lost.

These teachings are part of an ancient cultural heritage that hate-mongering radical-Right fundamentalism steadily erodes. It does so by appealing dangerously to the insecurities and deep fears that some people will inevitably feel amidst rapid cultural change and socioeconomic dislocation. Condemning others provides them with a false security or safety or status even as it erodes further the already deteriorating sense of national community.

Multiphrenia

Given a culture which demands that we "make something" of ourselves, given the loss of psychosocial security attendant upon living in a mobile, anonymous, urban society, we also face a third culturally unprecedented challenge. Personal identity must now be constructed amidst multiple, non-overlapping, swiftly changing social contexts. That can leave us with an oddly fractured sense of self.

Friedrich Schweitzer offers a great metaphor for the predicament we face. In *The Postmodern Life Cycle* (2004), he explains that identity can feel like a "construction site" where nothing is ever completed before remodeling begins. Our sense of self can seem to have something like competing "architects," each trying in a different way to adapt to one of our multiple social contexts.

In *The Self We Live By* (2000), James Holstein and Jaber Gubrium offer yet another compelling metaphor for the predicament we face: "multiphrenia." It's as if we have multiple selves, they argue. It's as if we have multiple identities, each relevant to its own high-pressure context, but no core self at all. We are not simply changing hats from one domain of our lives to another, they argue. We are changing heads. *My head spins,* we say. *My head feels like it's going to explode.* Even if then we laugh and get a grip and carry on, we are living day to day amidst a remarkable psychosocial challenge. *Who am I apart from all the roles that I play? Who am I apart from all my email accounts, my social media accounts, my job responsibilities, family responsibilities, professional identities, personal identities, my overlapping and non-overlapping social circles?*

Shame and Christian Fundamentalism

These cultural pressures explain why Christian humanism is potentially such a healthy and stabilizing force. Who I am "in the eyes of God" supersedes and transcends the psychologically fragmenting pressures of a postmodern, postindustrial society. By the same measure, however, this also explains why religious judgmentalism is so intimately destructive: people are told that who they are "in the eyes of God" is defective, deficient, morally outcast, and abhorrent, an accusation that can only be remedied by identifying with one's attacker and joining a hard-Right radical fringe.

"God" seems to have a very long "enemies list," one that overlaps in quite interesting ways with the enemies list of hard-Right libertarians. That hard-Right radical fringe has a fascinating history. As Princeton historian Kevin Kruse explains in *One Nation Under God: How Corporate America Invented Christian America* (2015), in the 1930s the business community and especially the financial sector were widely blamed for the Great Depression. In an effort both to defend themselves and to discredit the New Deal, major business figures channeled astounding amounts of money to Christian clergymen like James W. Fifield and Abraham Vereide. Fifield, Vereide, and others worked tirelessly and with considerable success to organize religious opposition to financial system regulations like the Glass-Steagall Act of 1933 and to progressive initiatives like Social Security, workplace safety legislations, and workers' right to unionize. All such efforts were condemned as "socialism." They were condemned as "anti-biblical." Under pressure from these campaigns, piety became ever more closely linked to hard-Right politics.

As these well-funded initiatives unfolded through the 1950s, piety and patriotism were also interwoven. "In God We Trust" was added to American currency; "under God" was added to the Pledge of Allegiance. But as Kruse documents in scholarly detail, the patriotism in question was unequivocally Right wing. These developments successfully swamped the "social gospel" movement from earlier in the century, a movement that had asserted Christian religious support for and concern about the poor, the economically exploited, the economically helpless, and so forth. That too was condemned as "socialism," especially when it resurfaced as "liberation theology," a movement originating in the 1950s and 1960s in the Catholic Church in South America.

In *With God on Our Side: The Rise of the Religious Right in America* (2005), William Martin essentially picks up the story from where Kruse concludes. As Martin documents in detail, the Religious Right arose in opposition to an array of politically progressive developments: the mid-1950s civil rights movement; the Civil Rights Act of 1964; desegregation of schools; equal rights for women; and especially the Supreme Court rulings in 1962 and 1963 against Christian prayer and Bible reading in public schools. These developments are the "big government" that the hard-Right fringe so vehemently opposes. Kruse adeptly labels this opposition "Christian libertarianism." That is no doubt a more accurate (albeit less familiar) label than "Religious Right."

By any label, however, these cultural developments reflect a political co-opting of Christianity that's no less dangerous than what happened in the Middle Ages under Charlemagne (detailed in *Confronting Religious Violence* and summarized below in chapter 6). As Christian humanist scholars can document in detail, these developments flatly contradict the authentic heritage of Jesus of Nazareth and biblical tradition properly understood.

There's an immense array of evidence I might bring to bear in supporting that claim. From amidst that array, I've chosen one small but cogent piece: the tale of Adam and Eve eating the forbidden fruit. In chapter 5 I'll take a very quick look at that famous story. But first let me tell a story of my own.

4

1960: What the Sky Seemed to Say

Growing up I remember being told—or at least *hearing*, which is of course quite different—I remember *hearing*, hearing repeatedly, that the first step toward a mature religious faith is to acknowledge and accept that I am sinner. *I am a sinner.* That's step one. *I am a sinner.*

And I remember a moment when I first began to question that teaching. I was probably ten years old, maybe eleven. Fifth grade, either late fall or early spring. My memories are anchored by bodily sensations: *it felt like this.* This memory feels like fifth grade.

Whatever age I was, I was walking south on Ridgeland Avenue in Oak Park, just four or at most five houses north of Harrison Street. I wasn't walking home from school. The memory doesn't feel like "walking home from school." It feels like going for a walk, walking south, wearing a tan corduroy coat with large square patch pockets, walking south to enjoy the late-winter or early-spring sun on my face. Given the angle of the light, given the level of energy I felt, it would have been at some point in the afternoon, that later-afternoon moment when energy starts to slow. The bare trees cast long lacy shadows. The lawns were grey-brown with only the palest, most uncertain blades of green here and there. I was going for an aimless walk. And I was thinking.

Or more precisely, thinking was happening to me. I was holding this idea that "I am a sinner" is the first step. I was just feeling that thought and walking, wordlessly, not arguing with the thought, just feeling it as I walked along, as I felt the pale sunlight, as I felt the lacy shadows of the trees, as I felt like whatever it felt like to be a girl my age, on the brink of puberty but only on the brink. Step one: *I am a sinner*. What does that thought feel like?

Nope, I decided. No. Maybe *I am a sinner* works somehow for them, but not for me. That didn't help to bring me closer to God. Or at least closer to this feeling of something warm and enormously bigger than I was. It knew me firsthand, as if the sky itself could see me right now if the sky could look down. Although the sky is huge, although the sky is over everything, if the sky could look down it could see me. Right?

The sky was partly overcast, those puffy clouds with dark bottoms and bright tops. The sky was huge. How could anyone know anything for sure about the sky?

I am a sinner didn't work for me. It made me feel bad. It made everything wrong that I had done feel bigger and worse, as if *not responsible about chores* or *not studying my spelling list* were the real truth about me. I knew that I did all of that. I also knew that I didn't feel as bad about not making my bed or not studying my spelling list as the grown-ups thought I should feel. I not only did not make my bed, I really didn't care about not making my bed. I also didn't care about spelling or long division, which I truly loathed. Even worse was calculating square roots. Those problems could consume an entire page of loose-leaf, my handwritten calculations smudged by repeated erasures and by my left-handedness. Why would anyone ever need the square root of 35,721?

I didn't care about any of it, not *any* of it, but I knew I was supposed to care. I also knew I was supposed to be both obedient and responsible. But I wasn't. I got away with as much as I possibly could. I was adept at getting away with things: grown-ups could be remarkably inattentive. I knew how much I got away with, even if the adults didn't know. But clearly they suspected. I knew they thought I was a problem. I heard them talking about not knowing what to do about me. I knew they all thought I should be different.

I also knew I *was* different. I knew I wasn't a bad girl. *Sinner* wasn't the truth about me. The truth about me was something else altogether. The truth was like something that only the sky could see, something that only the sky understood from way up there. Maybe from up there *everything* looked different.

Maybe for me that "first step toward a mature faith" was believing that only God understood the truth about me. Maybe only God understood who I was, who I really was, who I was that was more than this girl who couldn't spell, who couldn't multiply accurately, whose handwriting was careless, who didn't do her homework, who always got "fails to work up to potential" checked on her report cards, and whose chores were never completed to satisfaction. One Saturday I vacuumed the staircase four times. Somehow they still were not clean enough, and Mom was beside herself. I was wrong even when I was *trying* to do it right.

Adults were not the only problem. Other kids teased me for using big words. "Miss Dictionary," they called me. "The Brain." But words were words: words said what I needed to say or they didn't. Words didn't come in "sizes." I didn't know what I'd said that set them off. I never knew what I'd said. But when I was confused by their reaction, they'd all laugh even harder. And then the nun would get mad at *me* for making them laugh. But I wasn't a class clown, just as I wasn't disobedient and irresponsible. What was I to do? The nuns were trying to catch me not paying attention, because of course I wasn't paying much attention. What had they been talking about? I had to think fast. It was a stupid contest between the nuns and me. I always won this little game—I could see that flash across their faces—but saying anything under pressure and in front of other kids was a reliable disaster.

Despite how everyone else felt about me, everyone everywhere, I knew wasn't a bad kid. I was something else. To be that something else, to be something other than those bad feelings about how bad I was, I had to believe that God knew who I was, who I was deep down, who I was so deep down that I could only feel it, feel it as I could feel my heart beating or the air moving down into my chest, feel it like that. Not *I am a sinner* but *I am more than what you see. I am more than what I see* too.

That's the beginning, the sky seemed to say. *Start there.*

1960: WHAT THE SKY SEEMED TO SAY

The first step toward God for me, not for them maybe but for me, was trusting that I am what I am deep down, and God sees that too. Maybe only God sees it because God sees everything, things visible and invisible. That's what we say, "maker of all things, visible and invisible." The invisible me, the me I can only feel deep down, as I feel God deep down. Trusting that is the first step, not "I am a sinner."

These thoughts caught me up short. Suddenly I realized what I had been thinking. My surprise generated that brilliantly clear snapshot memory, frozen in time across more than fifty years, a visual and visceral memory of that particular spot on Ridgeland Avenue just north of Harrison Street, the bare trees, the gas station on the southeast corner of Ridgeland & Harrison, the pale sun reflecting off the smooth new pavement of the expressway overpass on the newly built interstate just south of Harrison Street. That moment: awake abruptly from a reverie spinning itself out in my mind.

I'm just a kid, I thought. *How can I think a thought this big? How can I question what they say about "I am a sinner"? I'm just a kid.*

But the big thought sat there, right there inside me. And I knew it was right. And I knew that this thought changed everything about what they said about God. Surely it changed more than I understood, because I was just a kid. What did I know?

If a thought can say to its thinker *that's okay, don't worry about them*, that's what the thought said, except it wasn't words at all. It was a feeling of *it's okay for them. Okay for them. Not for you, but that's okay. It's okay.*

"Grown-up business," my parents called it. All the time they said to me, "Don't worry about that, it's for grown-ups, it's not for kids. Stop asking questions. Go play. Don't worry about that."

And my felt sense of God got warmer and closer and more secure, even though God felt even more mysterious than ever, even though God felt immeasurably bigger than ever before. Maybe it was possible to be connected to God in more ways than I realized. Maybe there was *God's business* just as there was *grown-up business* and it was not for me to try further to figure it out. I knew that my job as a kid was to be obedient and to do what I was told and not to ask questions that it was not my place to ask, especially not when I had been told clearly—*told clearly*, that absolute category of adult demand—especially when I had been *told clearly* what to do.

And I had been told clearly: *I am a sinner* was not for me the first step toward relationship with God. Relationship with God ran in the opposite direction.

I knew about taking different directions. The other kids in the neighborhood walked home from school eastbound along Van Buren. That's how we were supposed to go, because that's where the crossing guards were at busy streets. But when other kids were giving me a bad time, I'd cut one block south to Harrison Street. I'd walk east on Harrison, not Van Buren. There were no other kids on Harrison Street. It was safe. Harrison was also sunnier in winter because of the new interstate under construction alongside it.

And so my way home was not the way home that the other kids took. But that was okay. Maybe from high enough up all these different routes made sense. And so maybe walking away from "I'm a sinner" was like walking home on Harrison Street. How other kids got home was not my business to worry about. I was only responsible for what I had been *told clearly* was my responsibility, which was *not*, absolutely *not* to think that *I am a sinner* would get me anywhere except into deeper trouble.

I was already in deep enough trouble. I was already in very deep trouble everywhere I looked. That was obvious. Everybody knew that. Everybody agreed on that. I knew it, the other kids knew it, all the adults knew it. I was trouble, I was in trouble, I was *not meeting expectations* on all sides, that black check mark on report cards visible and invisible.

Except maybe with God. God saw something else. God saw something I could not see. Maybe I couldn't see it but I could feel it, I could feel it way deep down, so deep down it was utterly invisible. But real. As God is real—a God who suddenly felt far more inexplicable than even than the adults seemed to understand.

That's okay, the sky seemed to say again. *Don't argue with them. Don't question them.* Asking questions would mean even more trouble, and I didn't need more trouble. I was simply to remember what I had been *clearly told* to do and to avoid what I had been *clearly told*

I should avoid. I was not to believe *I am a sinner*. And I was to avoid telling anybody about any of this.

I have only the faintest memory of turning eastbound onto Harrison Street. All I remember is the swing of my visual field to the east, the sun now on the right side of my face as the scene ends. Then the curtain of memory comes down with the absolute authority of black velvet, blocking my view of whoever I was then and whatever I did next.

I don't know what I did next. I don't remember whether this moment made any difference at all. I know that I never talked to anybody about any of it: as far as I recall, this is the very first time I've told anyone. And I know that all these familiar troubles persisted through high school: puberty does not make such a stubborn child more compliant.

More than fifty years later, however, I have strong opinions about this "I am a sinner" business. Maybe that claim works in healthy ways for some people, a possibility to which I will return in chapter 11. If it works in healthy ways for others, then that's okay for them. But it doesn't work in healthy ways for many of us. The claim that self-loathing is the first step toward God has done immense damage to many people.

And if I get into trouble today for saying so, then that's okay. I'm no longer a vulnerable child. And I learned how to survive such disapproval at a very early age.

And another thing: since then I've also learned that an immense and ancient theological tradition agrees with what the sky seemed to say that afternoon: "I am a sinner" is a step in the wrong direction.

5

Shame as a Moral Issue: The Forbidden Fruit

We have just hiked through some difficult terrain. I've raised some issues that are psychologically challenging for any of us. So let's stop here for a moment to catch our breath. If we were actually together, rather than "virtually" together, I'd make some strong black tea in my favorite red teapot, and I'd set out a plate of my raisin-oatmeal cookies (the King Arthur whole-wheat version that includes a little apple cider vinegar—somebody at King Arthur is clearly a candidate for sainthood). We need a break.

In lieu of a good cuppa tea, let me repeat here the major claims I have just laid out for your consideration.

It seems to me that the highly competitive American culture challenges each of us to (a) construct core identity and (b) to do so in isolation both from the cultural past and from a small, loyal, affirming community within which we work and live. And then, furthermore, (c) we need to prove the value of what we have constructed. Prove to whom? Prove to whomever. That's part of the problem: to whom are we struggling to prove ourselves? That's never entirely clear. And so there's never an entirely clear answer.

As a result, it's easy to feel lost in a fog of insanely perfectionist standards. But if we reject our own humanity, of course we doom ourselves to live in fear of rejection by others.

SHAME AS A MORAL ISSUE: THE FORBIDDEN FRUIT

In Christian humanist terms, we are doomed to struggle with shame because we fail to understand that in God's eyes we are *beautiful,* not *perfect.* We are made by love for love, not by static perfection for static perfection.

Even without fundamentalist church billboards proclaiming *God hates you,* the competitive American cultural context works against such recognitions. The American cultural context is a setup for incessant self-doubt even among the most stalwart. It's a setup for a quietly nagging sense of inadequacy. Shame (and not depression) is the core psychological affliction of American society. Depression is simply what follows when shame proves relentless.

Christianity and Shame

Unlike Christian humanism, some versions of Christianity intensify these difficulties. These versions of Christianity insist that we ought to be ashamed of ourselves. We are profoundly inadequate—not simply inept or slackers in some particular performance, but inadequate as human beings. We are morally inadequate in the eyes of God. We are intrinsically evil. Supposedly.

And we are rescued from this predicament, supposedly, by Jesus, who accepts and on our behalf absorbs the wrath of God. The brutal torture and slow death that Jesus endured spares those who believe in him from everlasting punishment by God for their moral inadequacy and shameful failures as human beings. Fundamentalists think this way, of course; but so do far too many other Christians, some of them politically progressive and quite open-minded. And so take note: I'm taking a stand here on a major in-house issue. Christian humanism has a very different view of God and a very different view of human nature. Our theological lineage is just as distinguished as theirs.

When our children were in college, they were repeatedly accosted by earnest young Christians eager to save them from eternal damnation by the crazy-violent vindictive God of this other theological tradition within Christianity. The more often this happened, the more angry and resentful our kids became at the claim, *you're damned, but hey, look at me, I can save you. Come to my church or go to hell.* Religious nonsense about Darwin or the Bible or gay people was bad enough. What was worse, in their eyes, was the personal arrogance of this religious judgmentalism. Christianity at street level, they angrily insisted, is not what I had been teaching them about Christianity. I should wake up. I should try walking across campus trying to shed one of these obnoxious kids.

Worst of all, my kids complained, worst of all, was how sweet and earnest and well-meaning these students were. They were not mean-spirited and malicious in the ways that ordinary social bullies always are. They were simply clueless. They were oblivious to the larger, logical, systematic implications of what they were saying about God and what they were saying about in-group/out-group boundaries between Christians like them and everybody else in the world. Jesus had saved them from the wrath of a judgmental God (supposedly), and that was all that mattered. They were recruiting for the Sky Bully gang because inside its boundaries they had found acceptance and affirmation. And, of course, cosmic authority to judge other people.

These campus crusaders had never stopped to ask whether we *need* to be saved from God. Maybe we need far more urgently to be saved from one another.

Jesus did not come to save us from God. He came to include the excluded and to rescue the shamed from their isolation. He welcomed those his own culture regarded as outcast. He welcomed the despised. He reached out to the unwanted, to the "failures," to the "morally unclean," telling them, insisting to them, that in fact they too are the beautiful and beloved children of God. He clarified ancient theological tensions in his own tradition to make a radical claim: *God does not condemn and exclude anyone, and neither should we.* Despite the scriptural heritage of ancient stories portraying God as a brutally violent warrior-king, in fact God is nonviolent. And God calls us to nonviolence, to non-harming, to radical hospitality toward one another. Jesus called his followers to a radical hospitality that was to mirror on earth the unconditional inclusivity and all-embracing compassion that God offers.

"Original Sin" and Shame in the Garden

In *Restoring the Shamed* (2012) Robin Stockitt traces the ancient theological roots of Jesus' outreach to the outcast, the failures, and the shamed. He provides solidly detailed scriptural evidence that *shame* and not *rule breaking* is the central moral issue in biblical tradition. He offers a brilliant literary-theological analysis of the great temptation scene in Genesis, that moment when the snake tempts Eve to eat the forbidden fruit (Gen 2:24–3:10).

The great temptation episode in Genesis is not supra-historical direct revelation from God about some "event" in human prehistory (see *Confronting Religious Absolutism* [forthcoming], chapters 6 and 7.) It's a psychologically acute, metaphorically dense *story*. It's a story told and retold over generations because it dramatizes something about human nature that we still struggle to understand: the origin of human wrongdoing. What's more, the story sets that portrait within a larger creation story flatly insisting that the world is good and we are good—and not simply good: we are made in the indelible image of God. How can that be possible? How can good and evil coexist within us as they do?

Let me tell you a story, the ancients said. *Let me tell you a story.* The story captures and stabilizes the paradox, holding it steady for our imaginative consideration, letting us look into it closely but without offering a sociological or neuroscientific or any other variety of theoretical explanation. Stories present; they dramatize. Stories do not *explain,* even though, by the end of a story, we may feel that we have a far clearer understanding of some aspect of the human condition.

And here's the story. God tells Adam and Eve not to eat the fruit of the tree of the knowledge of good and evil, "for in the day you eat of it you shall die" (Gen 2: 17, RSV). Adam and Eve eat the fruit anyhow. And they don't die. At least they don't die physically. They "die" in another sense, in a metaphoric sense that's still common among us. "I thought I'd die," we say of moments when we feel acutely embarrassed, inadequate, or exposed in all of our vulnerable imperfection. We feel *mortified,* we say, from *mort,* the French word for "death." So also for Adam and Eve: the immediate consequence of the fruit is not biological death. They were not poisoned, nor struck by lightening, nor did a flash flood drown the two of them. Instead they suffer an acute sense of shame.

References to "nakedness" permeate the story, because "naked" is its major metaphor for human vulnerability. To be "naked" is to be fully exposed to potential rejection, ridicule, or attack by others. To be naked is to lack defense, disguise, or protection against the critical judgment and potential hostility of others. In their initial nakedness, Adam and Eve do not fear that vulnerability: the story opens with the narrator pointing out that they were naked and not ashamed (Gen 2:25, RSV). "Naked" clues us that they do not judge, nor do they feel judged; they do not condemn, nor do they feel condemned. As a result, "naked" is not a problem. They are unselfconsciously self-accepting and they accept one another without question, doubt, or criticism.

But after eating the fruit of the tree of the knowledge of good and evil, that changes. Adam and Eve become ashamed of their nakedness. "Naked" now has a new meaning for them. Suddenly they are unwilling to face one another openly and vulnerably, and so they make clothes from fig leaves. Despite the fig-leaf coverings, they hide from God. They do not want God to see them just as they do not want to be fully seen by one another. They hide from God, we are told, not because they have broken the rule about the forbidden fruit, but because now they are ashamed and afraid of their naked, exposed humanity. That's a "nakedness" that fig leaves cannot fully remedy. Now they do feel judged, and so they fear the vulnerability to rejection that such judgment entails. "Naked" is no longer safe.

What has changed for Adam and Eve? That's the crucial question here. The usual legalistic answer is that they are overcome by a fully appropriate self-revulsion at having disobeyed God's edict about the forbidden fruit. That familiar interpretation validates the complaint that so many honest critics of Christianity have made over the years: Christianity teaches that shame, self-aversion, self-loathing, etc., are morally appropriate. We *should* be ashamed of ourselves, a teaching that many people (rightly) reject. Stockitt argues at length, and from a sophisticated theological analysis of many related biblical passages, that this familiar legalistic interpretation of the story is mistaken.

To figure out what has changed for Adam and Eve, we need to take a closer look at what has just happened. What is the temptation offered by the snake? Here's the text: "But the serpent said to the woman, 'You will not die. God knows that when you eat of it your eyes will be opened, and you will be like God, knowing good and evil'" (Gen 3:4-5, RSV). That is, the snake in effect says *You are not okay just as you are. You are not God. You lack divine powers. You are "blind" and God wants to keep you blind; God has lied to you in order to insure that you remain inferior to God. God is playing a one-upmanship game on you, and you are being a chump for not seeing through his strategy. But I know a way to fix all of that.*

In narrative terms, their eating the fruit is the plot action whereby the story indicates that they believe the snake's critical judgment about their present blindness and about God's fearful, jealous dishonesty. The snake invites them to reject their own humanity, to distrust God, and to become divine themselves. They agree. Their effort backfires. They feel diminished, not divinized. Their eyes are not opened to see as God sees; instead their vision is distorted by shame. If God himself is a jerk, then of course—by the same impossible yardstick, by the same misdirected critical intelligence—they feel like failures themselves. They feel defective and therefore afraid. They withdraw.

Seen in this light, God's warning them not to eat the fruit of the tree of the knowledge of good and evil is perhaps an honest warning about the dangers of moral judgmentalism whether directed against ourselves or against others. It is perhaps not unlike one's host for a weekend in the country warning about poison ivy in a particular ravine. Like Adam and Eve themselves, the world God has created is *good*, but it is by no means *perfect*. There are inescapable limitations. There are snakes; there's poison ivy; there's fruit that will make you feel utterly miserable if you eat it. Look out for those purple cherries: you won't believe what they will do to you. We need to live with these limitations wisely.

If we recognize that their eating the fruit is a symbolic action— evidence that they believe the snake—then everything else in the episode starts falling into place. The temptation episode portrays the tragedy of the human condition as our mistaken tendency to judge ourselves critically or to see ourselves as defective. That tendency is tragic because our compensatory efforts will inevitably fail. No matter what fig leaves we desperately clutch, no matter how earnestly we try to prove ourselves to this invisible self-critical judge, we cannot escape shame until we accept both our own limitations and the limitations of others. We have to recalibrate our critical intelligence away from the demand and the expectation that we can and should be divine, perfect, flawless, and perfectly in control of all things at all times (and, yes, popular and successful and admired and buff. Do not forget buff).

We also have to recalibrate our critical intelligence away from condemning others and plotting revenge against them. We must learn to forgive others for their fears and their failures, for their neediness and insecurities, for their self-obsessions, blindness, and all the wrongdoing that results. We must stop condemning and excluding others as harshly as if we were the controlling and condemning God portrayed by the snake. That's not who God is. That's not an authority we should pretend to claim. *Watch out for snakes peddling the poisonous fruit of suspicious, hostile judgmentalism.*

As the story unfolds, Adam and Eve are banished from what Stockitt calls the pre-cultural "garden" of pure unselfconscious confidence and secure, nonjudgmental relationships. Like the eating of the fruit, such exile dramatizes in external action the inward change in their psychological state. Before eating the fruit, they were told to tend the garden and to be fruitful and multiply. After eating the fruit—"outside" the garden of unselfconsciousness self-acceptance and nonjudgmentalism—the labor of farming and the labor of birthing both feel like punishment.

When we are trapped in shame, that's what happens: facts feel like punishments. Inevitable limitations feel like morally culpable failures for which we *should* be punished by a judgmental God. Everything that's difficult in our lives testifies further to our inadequacy, to our sense of failure and insignificance, to our sense that something is inexplicably *wrong* with us and with the lives we are

SHAME AS A MORAL ISSUE: THE FORBIDDEN FRUIT

leading. Instead of belonging and feeling securely loved, we feel ever more desperately isolated and angry. And so Adam and Eve's relationship with one another becomes inescapably troubled. When, later still, Adam and Eve have two sons, one kills the other out of jealousy regarding whose gift is more acceptable to God.

On the basis of this analysis and others like it, Stockitt argues persuasively that we should give up the usual religious focus on human mistakes or disobedience. Obsessing about the rules and breaking the rules serves only to blind us to shame as a moral issue pervading Scripture. As Stockitt points out, the relevant Hebrew word for shame, *bôsh,* appears in Scripture 128 times.[1] He offers rich, thought-provoking analyses of many specific scenes in Scripture dealing with shame and with facing or not-facing God, each time cycling back to the forbidden fruit episode as the mythic archetype of the psychological dynamics of self-aversion as a spiritual and moral issue.

And here's Stockitt's major conclusion: when Christians say that Jesus "takes away the sin of the world," the essential scriptural referent is to a healing or a cleansing from this dark, abiding sense of not good enough, not included, not beloved. Our misbehavior toward others arises primarily from our blind, mistaken efforts to "prove" ourselves, especially our efforts to prove ourselves superior to others. We misbehave—sometimes violently—from a need to compensate for intolerable feelings or perceptions that we are *unwanted, inadequate, contemptible, fraudulent,* or *inferior to others.* Those feelings are the "original" problem within the human condition. That's what this ancient story is trying to show us.

In short, we are all eating that forbidden fruit all of the time. We are all compensating—and overcompensating—for our own (often minimally conscious, always culture-specific) fears about not measuring up. We listen all too often to the snakey voice of self-ridicule, self-abuse, self-derision.

That's why "exile" is such central metaphor in the core biblical narrative: exile from Eden, exile in Egypt, exile in Babylon. Metaphorically speaking, to be exiled is to be subject to a relentlessly

---

1. Stockitt, *Restoring the Shamed,* 23.

critical judge to whom we can never prove ourselves. Our distorted moral judgment serves only to drive us deeper into social isolation and the alienation of self-aversion, self-unworthiness, and self-condemnation. "Naked" will never feel safe: we will always need disguises, defenses, protective gear. We will never feel "at home," with all the safety and security that "home" archetypally invokes. We feel banished from the garden in which we once somehow did feel secure. And in our exile from that secure self-acceptance, we are deeply tempted to judgmental condemnation of everyone around us.

Spiritually speaking, morally speaking, biblical "exile" is this hall of mirrors in which we feel incessantly judged and we no less incessantly judge others. We do so because "here"—wherever "here" is—we are estranged from the people around us. Our default relationship to others is compare, contrast, and compete. Shame or exile is the experience or the perception that we do not exist in relationships of mutual belonging-to and loyalty-from the people around us. In the absence of such relationships, we do not feel safe.

And not feeling "safe" is remarkably dangerous. Under threat, any animal behaves in unpredictable, often quite violent ways. Religious judgmentalism amplifies that threat by siding with the snake, telling us that we truly are inadequate and God is indeed out to get us.

Come to church or go to hell.

Antidotes to Shame: Radical Hospitality

Scripture attests that shame is a centrally important human predicament. And the ordinary social bully exploits our ordinary human liability to shame. He gives it voice. *You are the unwanted one. You are the excluded one. You do not belong. We would all be better off without you. You are the problem here.* That kind of malice drives adolescents to suicide. And the religiously judgmental, even when they are neither hostile nor malicious in any personal way, raise the stakes exponentially by claiming, like the snake in the garden, to have an answer: *You are damned. God himself condemns you. But we have the answer: repent, conform, come to our church! Worship the God of wrath and condemnation, and he might relent. He might exempt you from his plans to punish all of humanity as unworthy and unacceptable.*

That's a poisonous fruit. It's poisonous because the world remains divided between the saved and the damned. God remains the cosmic Border Guard separating us from them. And they will eventually be punished as brutally as they deserve, because the defective ones deserve physical pain as excruciating as the psychological pain of ridicule, derision, and rejection. The judgmentalism of the bully will one day be completed or physically externalized as the torture and death of the outcasts. (Cue up the book of Revelation.)

That telling of the story breaks my heart. That's not what church is about. It's not what healthy Christian community actually offers. Quite the contrary: faith as I understand it and as I have experienced it offers a potent antidote to shame. Christian faith is not the only antidote, of course. There are many antidotes to shame, just as there are many sources of shaming. But Christianity derives from a tradition that has spent thousands of years mulling over the problem of shame and the consequences of shame. It seems to me that Christianity and the God proclaimed by Jesus provide an intrinsic antidote to the shame, the second-guessing, and the self-doubt that are so inevitable for big-brained social obligates that have both flexible behavior and critical intelligence.

This antidote is simple: we are loved by God. We have nothing to prove to God. We are frail and fearful and limited, and hence psychological suffering is inevitable; but even in these limitations we are acceptable, worthy, and "enough." We were not created morally perfect, nor perfectly wise, nor were we given perfect control of all things at all times (much less perfect self-control). But we *were* created capable of love. Despite our imperfections, we were created capable of authentic, compassionate relationship both with God and with others.

Relationship with God can slowly transform how we see ourselves. It can be healing, just as loving human relationships can be healing. Such healing is an important step toward the practice of radical hospitality. As our own shame, self-aversion, and self-criticisms subside, we can begin to learn to accept, forgive, understand,

and love others in all of their imperfections. Accepting the limitations and the suffering of others is far healthier than blaming them, besting them, berating them, and everything else that humans do to silence our own demons of shame, self-doubt, and self-aversion. And as we endeavor to live in this way with others, we slowly but steadily grow in our perception of a relationship with a loving God. We stop grasping at the fig leaves of excuse-making, perfectionism, overwork, hostile competitiveness, and so forth. It's not Edenic. But it is human.

And it is *humane*.

―

Here's the bottom line, at least as I see it. Shame will always be a threat for all of us because we are social obligates who have highly developed neocortices. As a result, we have both a biological need to monitor our relationships with others and an exquisite ability to do so. We track how we are perceived by others around us even when others are ignoring us, because in its own way that's quite threatening too. Shame and its opposite, secure and loyal belonging, are inescapably primal concerns no matter how staunchly "independent" or "individual" or "self-realized" our culture tells us we ought to be.

Culture cannot turn intensely social human beings into the psychosocial equivalent of solitary condors or thick-shelled sea turtles. Unlike condors and sea turtles, we do not float alone through life, encountering others only for a rare moment of mating. For social obligates like us, shame and secure inclusion are hardwired anxieties because isolated individuals are easy prey for predators. Even in the absence of saber-toothed tigers, and as Norman Anderson documents in *Emotional Longevity* (2003), socially isolated people die much younger than socially integrated individuals.

At its best, Christianity offers radical hospitality as an antidote to shame. At its best, Christianity insists that we are exquisitely and unbelievably cherished by God exactly as we are, right here and now. God sees us as beautiful despite our self-doubts, because only God sees the fullness of our humanity. We don't see it, or we see it only in glimpses. If we trust God and God's vision of us, Christian wisdom insists, then we will slowly feel less liable to the doubts and the fears that fuel shame and hence the toxic varieties of status-seeking. We will be far less tempted to promote or to defend ourselves at someone else's expense.

And that raises an obvious question: where did this toxic religious judgmentalism come from? That's a great question. The short answer is that these teachings are tough-minded. They are difficult to sustain. Like the other major global religions, Christianity offers ideals that are intended for self-aware grown-ups. And so, like every other religious tradition, Christianity has been at times misunderstood, corrupted, co-opted manipulatively, and so forth.

The long answer is a very long story indeed. But in the next chapter I will offer a plot summary of what happened. What happened back then matters because this co-opting continues right under our noses today.

6

From Judgment to Judgmentalism: Some Quick History

I've been complaining repeatedly that fundamentalist judgmentalism represents the loss of a nuanced and valuable moral heritage. In this chapter, I want to begin to put some meat on the bones of that complaint.

Christian judgmentalism is rooted in two theological mistakes. The first mistake was redefining God as a condemning and controlling judge determined to punish humanity for our sinfulness. As I explain in detail in *Confronting Religious Violence*, that happened in the 800s under the emperor Charlemagne. The second mistake was redefining the Bible as an empirically grounded, historically accurate account of God's actions and statements to humanity. That happened in the nineteenth century as a reactionary denial of scholarly developments in three fields: geology, biology, and biblical studies. I tell that story in detail in *Confronting Religious Absolutism* [forthcoming].

Here I want to focus more narrowly, asking a more specific, more down-to-earth question: how do these two theological mistakes distort moral judgment? How do these mistakes encourage people to be harshly judgmental in their own personal and political lives? And—perhaps most important of all—what ancient wisdom did these theological mistakes obscure?

FROM JUDGMENT TO JUDGMENTALISM: SOME QUICK HISTORY

Moral Law and Ancient Narratives

Morally offensive religious judgmentalism often derives from biblical literalism and its companion theories, biblical inerrancy and papal infallibility. So let's start here with misreading Scripture.

You don't have to become Christian to recognize that storytelling is a rich and subtle basis for teaching morality. The story of the boy who cried "Wolf!" is more effective by far than repeating over and over again the simple moral edict "Do not lie." *Do not lie* is the "moral" of the story or it's "theme," of course. It's a simple tale with a simple message, suitable for children. The richer, more elaborate storytelling of Scripture offers far more complex insight into the human condition. It does so by exploiting every subtle resource of the storytelling art. That subtlety is lost—and with it wisdom is lost—when stories are reduced to bare news reporting.

In *Scripting Jesus: The Gospels in Rewrite* (2010), biblical scholar L. Michael White explains a crucially important scholarly consensus: in the ancient world of the Mediterranean basin, morality was taught by telling stories. In the ancient world, morality was not conceptualized as a self-consistent rational system derived from self-evident first premises. Morality was what moral people *did*. Understanding the logic behind their actions was important, of course, but it had a derivative importance. Good people were not simply following good rules. Good behavior arose from good *character*. And good character was shaped by the hearing and the telling of stories, not by studying rule books.

As a result, major religious traditions globally commonly include collections of ancient stories about moral exemplars and their heroic adventures. Amidst his epic trek leading the Jews from slavery to the promised land, Moses spends time in the cloud-wrapped Mount Sinai taking moral instruction from God himself. In Buddhism, Siddhartha Gautama sets out from his father's castle, achieves enlightenment and nirvana, and then returns to earth as the Buddha because he wants to relieve the suffering of humanity. Socrates is executed by the state for arguing that the Homeric epics fail to provide adequate moral instruction to the young, but Plato, his student, promptly transforms Socrates into a new-and-improved heroic moral exemplar. Plato's stories about Socrates's conversations and confrontations are still studied in philosophy courses. In Hinduism, Prince Arjuna has a long argument about the meaning of life with the god Vishnu, disguised for the moment as the warlord Krishna.

Jesus is born in a stable, confronts the powers that be, consoles the outcast and the economically exploited. He knows he will be crucified sooner or later for his witty, subversive confrontation with Roman imperial ideology, and so he chooses the timing of his inevitable death. He does so to make the strongest possible theological claim to all the Jews gathered in Jerusalem for Passover: *God is not violent. God does not even take revenge for the death of the Messiah.* Rising on the third day, he sends his followers out to continue building small, subversive communities of radical hospitality and inclusion. And so forth. In classical and preclassical antiquity, and even as late as Mohammed (roughly 600 CE), morality derived from the achievements and teachings of a heroic figure.

Why was this the case? Why this emphasis on heroic biography? Here's why: in the ancient world, both political authority and intellectual authority were vested in persons, just as morality was grounded in narratives. One did not owe political or intellectual allegiance to a system of law, much less "law" itself as a concept. One owed allegiance to a *personal relationship*. (Much of the non-Western world still thinks this way.) All authority was personal, just as all moral teachings were embedded within narratives and not within self-evident logical systems. The moral hero biography brought these two beliefs together into a single text.

In short: the moral hero biography was a major literary convention in the ancient world. To speak from a twenty-first-century literary perspective, heroic biography was the literary means whereby a long and influential cultural era signaled that a given set of teachings had authority, truth value, ethical stature, and so forth. *That's how they did it.* They preserved their most important moral insights by telling stories about moral heroes because stories are both more flexible and far more durable than any theory out there. These stories have survived across thousands of years.

FROM JUDGMENT TO JUDGMENTALISM: SOME QUICK HISTORY

And why have they survived? First, because they are great stories in their own right, and we love a great story. Second, they have survived because stories are how the human mind organizes and remembers the very most complex kinds of information. Identity itself is a story, according to personality psychologist Dan McAdams.[1] Roger Schank, a pioneer in artificial intelligence, argues that *meaning* of any kind is a story.[2] Cultural historian Stephen Prickett contends that even the most rigorous scientific research paper tells a story: I asked, I tested, I found.[3] As Jonathan Gottschall argues in *The Storytelling Animal* (2012), if you want to make an idea stick, tell a story about it. The reverse is also true, I'd suggest: great stories keep their ideas alive, because we will retell a great story for its own sake. In short, the ancients had a point when they insisted that morality is transmitted by the hearing and the telling of stories, not by or through logically self-consistent, philosophically rigorous theorizing about morals. *Of course* the survival of a religion depends upon the skill of its storytellers. And the Jewish storytellers were world class.

As a Christian humanist—and a professionally trained literary critic—I want to reclaim and to protect the moral brilliance and stunning wisdom of these stories *as stories*. As stories they are part of the global cultural and moral heritage, just as ancient temples and cathedrals are. Like the immense heritage of classical music and visual art composed for religious purposes or on religious themes, these stories are deeply moving creative achievements. You don't have to convert to Christianity to see and to value this heritage, just as you don't have to join any other religion to marvel at and to be moved by its ancient monuments and classic wisdom about the human condition.

---

1. McAdams, *The Stories We Live By*.
2. Schank, *Tell Me a Story*.
3. Prickett, *Narrative, Religion, and Science*.

How Literalism Leads to Judgmentalism

The problem, of course, is that beginning roughly between 1870 and 1890, this complex literary heritage was reread as a literal and infallibly accurate account of historical events. Adam and Eve were real people; so were Noah, his family, and his ark full of animals. The walls of Jericho fell when Joshua blew his horn, the Red Sea parted when Moses held up his hand, Jesus walked on the water, and so forth.

These stories, transformed into literal accounts of "actual events," were furthermore defined as culturally transparent and exempt from the vicissitudes of cultural change. "Walking on the water," for instance, means *walking on water,* plain and simple. Jesus had the power to change the surface tension of water, period. This is an *event,* not a metaphor, a symbol, an allusion, or anything like that. As a result, the "walking on water" story needs no "interpretation" (supposedly).

In effect, "no interpretations" is a major interpretation, one that's particularly difficult to defend. Even more oddly, at least from a Protestant point of view, biblical literalism and biblical inerrancy in effect say to the rest of us, "You can't read the Bible for yourself. You can only read the Bible as we tell you to. You can't bring to bear your own common sense, your own historical sense, your own sensitivity to cultural context, your own literary sensibilities. You can't bring to bear whatever you have learned about what biblical scholars have discovered about the circumstances in which these stories were told and then written down and then—against all odds—copied and recopied in secret and by hand for generations. Forget all that. Read as we tell you to read."

This literalism arose in opposition to biblical scholarship originating with the first Christian humanists in the 1300s, a scholarly tradition that was particularly vibrant in Germany in the 1700s and 1800s. As I explain in *Confronting Religious Absolutism,* developments in geology and biology were threatening to the biblical literalists, but science was a secondary threat. The bigger threat came from biblical scholars. Scientists simply confirmed what these Christian humanist biblical scholars had been saying for centuries: despite

FROM JUDGMENT TO JUDGMENTALISM: SOME QUICK HISTORY

naïve popular assumptions, Genesis is not a record of historical events; neither is Noah's flood. And so forth.

As the Christian humanists had discovered, no one in the ancient world would have read such stories literally. Philo of Alexandria, who was a generation or so older than Jesus of Nazareth, had reinterpreted the entire Exodus narrative in allegorical terms as an account of the spiritual journey of the soul toward maturity. And that was typical of how these very ancient tales were understood. The "literal" meanings of the stories were trivial at best. But this ancient understanding of Scripture was lost when the Roman Empire became a failed state in the 400s. Recovering this intellectual heritage was the first and most stunning achievement of the original Christian humanists.

I have much more to say about biblical literalism, biblical inerrancy, and papal infallibility is *Confronting Religious Absolutism* [forthcoming], chapters 6–8. For present purposes, what matters is that biblical literalism in effect erased biblical stories *as stories*. Christianity was instead recast as a rigidly punitive legal system, which in turn gives rise to religious judgmentalism. This system was supposedly derived from "empirical" events in the Bible, from comments made by the stories' narrators, and from dialogue among biblical characters. These events, comments, and dialogues were recast as unquestionable truth claims true in all circumstances everywhere.

When the Bible is understood as an absolute source of unquestionable moral requirements and prohibitions (or when "the church" is regarded as literally infallible, which is the fundamentalist-Catholic equivalent of biblical literalism and inerrancy), then individual believers are in effect handed a set of claims that are something like nuclear weapons. These are claims that cannot be used without poisoning the intellectual environment.

That happens in two ways. First, individuals are no longer responsible for evaluating the justice, propriety, or evidential basis of their claims and their attacks on others: *the Bible says it, I believe it, that settles it.* (Or, for equally fundamentalist Catholics, *The church says it, I believe it, that settles it.*) It's pointless to argue with such people that they are ignoring empirical evidence on the issue at hand or imposing their own religious beliefs upon others. *Of course they are*. In their eyes, that's entirely appropriate. They and they alone have the God-given truth, straight from the hand of God himself. The claim that "here is absolute unquestionable truth" tempts individuals to tyrannical, judgmental, and antisocial behavior—behavior supposedly demanded by that cosmic condemning Father with his terrifying threat of eternal torment.

Second, individual believers are expressly forbidden to question these sweeping condemnations no matter how irrational, unjust, and morally repugnant the outcomes. That's explicitly anti-intellectual. It's explicitly *reactionary* in the most negative sense of that term: it's a setup for morally irresponsible authoritarianism. It's an invitation to tyranny.

Such co-opting or corruption or misappropriation or "hacking" of the tradition has happened repeatedly in the past. Reasonable Christians have been fending it off from the beginning. That's a fascinating story, one that I tell in much greater detail in *Confronting Religious Violence*, chapters 5–9. Here I want to offer an exceedingly brief plot summary of what happened when Christianity became the state religion of the Roman Empire.

The Politically Useful God of Condemnation and Control

Reading the Bible literally—as an accurate record of historical events involving God—creates major theological problems, because the Bible portrays "God" in strikingly contradictory ways. At times "God" is a savage warrior and brutally controlling monarch willing to slaughter his own people to insure their unquestioning obedience. At other times, "God" is portrayed no less vividly as compassionate "Presence" calling us to compassion with one another. He yearns to embrace all of humanity in his loving-kindness, and he promises repeatedly that some day everyone everywhere will realize this fact. The God of compassionate presence would never behave as brutally as God the savage warrior-king. So who is God?

The tension between these two versions of God permeate Hebrew Scripture from the first pages of Genesis. The tension was briefly resolved by the teachings of Jesus that God is compassionate

FROM JUDGMENT TO JUDGMENTALISM: SOME QUICK HISTORY

and therefore systematically nonviolent. But that resolution didn't hold, or it didn't hold for long. Perhaps it didn't hold because in the face of vicious Roman persecutions at least some Christians gave way to fantasies of violent revenge, violent fantasies like what we see in the book of Revelation. Perhaps it didn't hold because universal compassion is a difficult teaching. For sure it didn't hold because Christianity eventually became the official state religion of the Roman Empire. Rome needed a violent, controlling warrior God, because such a God is politically useful.

Historians and sociologists of religion might have predicted that Jesus' teachings about God would be corrupted this quickly and this extensively. So let's pause here just for a few minutes for a quick survey of how sociologists would view the enduring theological contest between these two very different visions of God.

In the ancient Near East, and often globally as well, kings and emperors were accountable to no one. Kings and emperors had an authority that was beyond question. The sociological function of religion in these societies was to validate and ritually to celebrate the authority of those in authority. The role of religion was to affirm the legitimacy of the elite—the economic elite, the social elite, and the political elite. And these elites were, of course, essentially one group, even though individuals within the group regularly vied for power with one another (just as they do today).

In the ancient Near East, Jewish tradition was distinctively quirky on this issue. They were outliers. In Hebrew Scripture, the Jewish king was not morally absolute in the usual sense. Quite the contrary. The Jewish king was accountable to God and to God's laws as given to Moses. Kings were regularly—and scathingly—called into account by prophets who condemned them for neglecting the needs of the economically helpless, for exploiting the labor of the poor and landless, for siding with the wealthy elite against the common good of the whole society, and so forth. The Jesus Movement, in its radical claims about Jesus as the legendary "Messiah," sided with and exponentially advanced the moral demands of the classic Jewish prophetic tradition: the king is accountable to God, who demands both responsibility to the common good ("loving our neighbors as ourselves") and generous hospitality for the helpless, the unemployable, the immigrant, and the stranger. Everyone gets a place at the table, enough to eat, and clean water to drink. I explain the Jesus movement in much more detail in *The Confrontational Wit of Jesus: Political Satire in the Gospels* [forthcoming], especially chapter 3, "The Moral Imagination of Jesus."

As a result, early Christianity existed in remarkable tension with what the pagan Gentile world expected from a religion. How can a religion be *countercultural*? How can a religion question and challenge the socioeconomic status quo? That's why Christians were persecuted by the empire until the early 300s CE. But beginning in the 300s, as Christianity slowly moved into place as the "official" or state-sponsored religion of the Roman Empire, this potent, classically Jewish moral vision clashed with the ruthless political requirements of empire as usual.

In 381–82 CE, the Roman emperor Theodosius I established Christianity as the sole legitimate religion of the Roman Empire. At that point, "Christian orthodoxy" became a measure of loyalty to the emperor or to regional governors. "Heretics" were "treasonous" and they were treated as such. In effect (sweeping generalization alert), Theodosius's decrees set off an epic clash between *hospitality* and *hostility* as the "brand identity" of Christian community. For present purposes, here's what matters: for the next thousand years or so, the inherently subversive, resolutely nonviolent God of compassionate loving-kindness had to contend with the politically more useful God of command, control, and condemn. The teachings of Jesus had to contend with the ideological needs of empire, for whom a fiercely judgmental God was far more useful. A violent, judgmental God provided crucial cosmic legitimacy for the violence of imperial policy, because a violent God both sanctifies and sanctions human violence. That's what the Roman Empire needed its state religion to provide.

Charlemagne and Atonement Theology

Here's the key episode in that thousand-year contest for control of the Christian "brand." In the early 800s CE, the emperor Charlemagne demanded—and got—key changes to the major Christian worship service. Prior to these changes, the altar had been symbolically identified as a banquet table. Here was the cosmic feast of the kingdom of God: everyone is welcome and no one leaves hungry; if we share equitably, there's enough to go around. But after Charlemagne, the altar was symbolically redefined as a butcher block. Jesus the Lamb of God was ritually slain every Sunday, a brutal human sacrifice to calm the wrath and assuage the injured dignity of God the Almighty.

In these changes, the savage torture and slow excruciating death of Jesus moved to center stage in the Christian moral imagination: Jesus absorbed the wrath of God on your behalf; be grateful, because otherwise God will do this to you—and worse—for an eternity, not for a few hours. These liturgical changes provided theological cover for Charlemagne's equally savage military campaign against the Saxons, who were "converted" at sword's point. Such violence flatly contradicted the teachings of Jesus, and so it took almost 300 years for this extraordinarily violent God to be fully reconciled with other aspects of Christian teachings. But that reconciliation was eventually worked out, most famously by Anselm of Canterbury in about 1100.

Atonement theology is a complex position whose failures I address in *Confronting Religious Violence,* chapters 8 and 9, and again in the "Postscript" to my introduction to this series, available on my author website, CatherineMWallace.com. What matters here, for our present focus on judgmentalism, is this: atonement theology defines God as the consummate cosmic judge. It portrays God as deeply committed to the violent condemnation and vicious physical punishment of sinful humanity. And despite the death of Jesus, the vast majority of humanity is doomed by the will of God to suffer eternally.

That theology is politically dangerous. It's culturally dangerous. It's also remarkably common, and not simply among hard-Right politicized fundamentalists. Disagreements about atonement theology run deep within contemporary Christianity: I am on one side of a major dispute.

I am on this side because I have been persuaded by evidence offered by generations of scholars that Jesus proclaimed the radical nonviolence of God. I have also been persuaded by cultural-theological historians tracing the consequences of Charlemagne's impositions upon Christian worship. In *Saving Paradise* (2003) Rita Nakashima Brock and Rebecca Ann Parker argue that the violent, vindictive God imagined by Charlemagne's liturgical changes provided theological justification for crusades, inquisitions, and some of the worst abuses of colonialism. In their earlier book, *Proverbs of Ashes* (2001), they offer an equally convincing critique of how belief in a violent, judgmental God has underwritten our abuse of one another. These two books are painful reading, but their theological clarity is extraordinary.

If God condemns anyone to eternal agony (or even to the cosmic equivalent of solitary confinement), then we are surely justified in condemning one another. All we need is a willingness to claim *Gott Mit Uns*, "God with Us," the legend engraved on the belt buckles of German soldiers in World War I and World War II.

But by equal measure, as a Christian humanist I refuse to surrender the grandly creative Jewish God of loving-kindness and social justice. That God was reclaimed and retaught by Jesus of Nazareth, who in classic prophetic ways confronted the collaborationist toadies of his own day, men who were allowing their proud and ancient faith to be co-opted by Roman colonial authorities. Jesus insisted that we must be courageously inclusive, personally generous, and programmatically non-harming. As we face the immense political, economic, and environmental problems of our own day, we need every possible cultural resource for teaching and for understanding what it might mean to reorganize both our lives and our society in these profoundly prosocial ways. Christianity is not the only source of insight into our predicament. But it's a major source.

And it must not be lost, nor twisted into rigid, narrow-minded, antisocial judgmentalism.

7

Where Do We Look?

Charlemagne's theology set the stage for the West's terrible Wars of Religion between 1524 and 1660. In just one thirty-year stretch (1618–1648), a greater percentage of Europe's people died than would later die in World War I and World War II *combined*. Almost twice as many, in fact. As a result, by the mid-1600s European intellectuals were desperate for a moral foundation that did not derive from Christianity. They sought a new foundation because now—thanks to Charlemagne—Christianity itself had proved politically unstable. At the theological level, Christianity now encouraged people to demonize and even to kill those with whom they disagreed. Classic Western-Christian moral judgment had deteriorated into politically dangerous moralistic judgmentalism.

Like many of today's "religiously unaffiliated" and "spiritual but not religious," these Enlightenment intellectuals did not object to the idea of God, to the practice of "prayer," or to the teachings of Jesus. They objected to the misuse of religion, not to religion itself. They objected to how ambitious clerical bureaucrats and clerical politicians had tried to reorganize "organized religion" for their own crass and self-serving ends. They sought a moral foundation for a sane and peaceful society, a moral foundation that did not allow these meddling, dangerous "churchmen" to dictate political policy.

They found that basis in a key teaching of Christian humanism: human critical intelligence is the light of God shining through us, just as human compassion is God's love flowing through us. Human rationality is to be trusted because its origins are sacred. It is a sacred gift. Critical intelligence is part of the divine image, the *imago dei*, found in everyone. We need to trust our brains, not the bishops.

If we are going to confront religious judgmentalism in our own day, we too need an intellectually solid understanding of authentic moral judgment. How *do* we know what's right? How *do* we properly decide what's right and what's wrong? If we can't clearly distinguish between right and wrong, then judgment is never anything more than judgmentalism. It's never anything more than the will to power, or, as my son said so many years ago, "just an opinion."

This is, of course, one of the biggest philosophical issues in Western tradition. With due deference to the saints and the scholars who have preceded me, I want to begin with this simple distinction (filched, I admit, from Thomas McFarland's magisterial *Coleridge and the Pantheist Tradition* [1969]): if we want to know what's right and what's wrong, if we want to acquire or to refine a mature moral judgment, either we look around or we look inside. We look around at our social context; we look inside to our own moral compass. We are empirical or we are introspective. Roughly speaking (sweeping generalization alert), moral thinkers can be sorted into one category or the other. So can most of us, I suspect. As I said, we already have opinions on these matters, whether or not our opinions are fully conscious.

Each approach to moral judgment succeeds in part, and in part each approach fails. That's the human predicament: there are no easy answers to our deepest question, "How, then, shall I behave?" *How shall I live my life?* Given our massive neocortex, given our remarkably flexible behavior, "How do I handle this?" matters acutely because there are so many possible answers.

In this chapter, I'll explain *look inside* and *look around* one at a time. Once that much is reasonably clear, I'll pull the camera back for a wide-angle look at how *in* and *around* also informed the great Enlightenment quest to understand moral judgment as something far more subtle than obedience to bishops or Bibles (chapters 7 and

8). Then and only then will I try to explain what I mean when I say that Christian humanism defines conscience as a creative process. In this creative process, we synthesize what we discover by looking inside with what we discover by looking around. Conscience as I understand it grapples honestly with the inevitable paradoxes of this double vision.

Looking Around

If we decide how to behave primarily by looking out at the world around us, we do so seeking what Aristotle called "the opinions of the many and the wise." We look around for social consensus and for the opinions of our peers. We look to our moral and religious heritage from the cultural past. What actions have had what consequences, and how do good people whom we trust evaluate those consequences? What measures do they use? How will people react if I do *this* rather than *that*? Looking around is one quite reasonable response. That's why we read consumer reviews of coffee pots, or subscribe to Angie's List, or talk to our friends: smart people have a reasonable respect for other people's critical thinking.

Our ability to look around arises from our remarkable neurological complexity: we are capable of *imagining* others' perspectives, others' needs, others' expectations of us, and the prerequisites of others' well-being. In *Primates and Philosophers: How Morality Evolves* (2006), animal ethnologist Frans deWaal argues that a capacity for prosocial behavior has evolved in tandem with increasing neurological complexity. He tells charming but pointed stories about primate behavior that is rightly called "animal morality," a capacity present to varying extents in social animals depending upon their brain structures. To some very real extent, a capacity for morality is hardwired into us as neurologically complex social obligates. Furthermore, our behavior is famously flexible, which makes possible intricate collaboration, which explains our ability to adapt collectively to environments as different as Alaska, the Amazon rainforest, and the Arabian deserts. How is all this collaborative adaptability possible? *We are capable of looking around, checking with others verbally and nonverbally, assessing our choices in subtle ways, and then adapting our behavior to what we discover.*

Neurologist Marco Iacoboni takes all of this a quantum leap forward in *Mirroring People: The New Science of How We Connect with Others* (2008). He describes "mirror neurons," which are brain cells found mostly in the motor cortex. If you scowl at me, or if you look puzzled or confused, I can pick up what you are feeling because some teensy fraction of my own motor neurons nudge individual muscle fibers in my face toward the same expression. Even if the expression on my face does not visibly change, I can literally *feel* what you are feeling.

Nonetheless, looking around at others' behavior sometimes fails quite remarkably as a guide to morality. Consider this: social consensus once endorsed slavery and the casual murder of unwanted daughters, whose tiny bodies routinely clogged the sewers of ancient cities. Social consensus still endorses a global economic system predicated upon factories run with slave labor or something close to slave labor. "Economic development" remains a global economic imperative even when it involves extraordinary environmental damage. There's nothing realistic we can do, we say. That's just how things are. We might regret this human suffering in a vague and general sort of way, but mostly we turn a blind eye to the real costs of whatever goods are in our shopping bags. We do so because it seems that we have no choice. (From what I can tell, every electric coffee maker in America is made in China.) No doubt this is how our ancestors felt discarding unwanted daughters, using slaves, or suffering enslavement. This is how the world is. There's nothing anyone can do to change this state of affairs. Give up. Give in. Go along.

That's how *look around* can trap us into mindless conformity. *Looking around* can leave us painfully lost and, alas, morally isolated from those around us.

Looking Inside

There is another option we might take as we try to decide how we ought to behave or how we ought to lead our lives: *look inside* ourselves. Decide what's right by reference to our own inner moral compass. Decide for ourselves what's right, no matter what other people might endorse or at least tolerate. Alas, this option is no less problematic than *look around*.

But *look inside* has its appeal. It has deep and rich value. We need to see that clearly before we examine its limitations.

Individual moral accountability is a major Christian belief, and so it lies deep in Western culture. Individual moral accountability is also a major component of individualism, which is a major Western trait and particularly central to American culture. Individual moral accountability also has an acute sensitivity to context—an empirical bias—that accords well with a high-tech society. Furthermore, individual moral accountability was strongly affirmed by the Nuremberg Trials of Nazi war criminals after World War II. "Just following orders," the tribunal ruled, is no defense. We are accountable for our own actions, regardless of "orders" and regardless of the social consensus of those around us.

And so we admire those morally courageous people who think for themselves and stand up against a social consensus. Every cultural moment has its array of such people. When over time these individuals prevail in changing a social consensus, they are hailed as prophets and moral heroes. But when they fail, they are dismissed as quixotic cranks. Or they are condemned as subversive, a condemnation that can lead to death. In any given moment, it can be remarkably difficult to separate the cranks from the heroes. How can we do so, after all, except by reference to our own inward moral compass?

Here's the problem: as everyone knows, the moral compass is to some indefinable extent shaped by how we were socialized growing up. Furthermore, and no matter what we do, no matter what choice we make, we know that somebody somewhere might ridicule us. No wonder we feel stressed. No wonder we struggle with self-aversion. *Looking inside* can leave us facing an abyss of self-doubt and defensive egotism. And this state of affairs perpetuates itself: insecurity and incessant self-criticism flips easily into an equally incessant criticism of others, online flameouts, bullying, and so forth. Criticizing others can be a dysfunctional way of affirming myself. *I am not like them. They are the problem. Not me. I am okay.* When such behavior shames and excludes others, they can be provoked into fighting back or bullying someone else. And so the cycle continues.

Self-aware individuals intuitively recognize that such attacks are a sign of insecurity and self-doubt. Such attacks are also a sign of moral rigidity, the kind of moral rigidity which denies the complexity of other people's lives and situations. Complexity can be denied because it is overwhelming, whether that's intellectually overwhelming or psychosocially overwhelming.

But recognizing that fact doesn't make any of it less overwhelming. The result has been called *normal nihilism*.

Normal Nihilism

Whether we look *around* or we look *inside,* it seems that all we find are predicaments heaped upon predicaments. And so we all too easily default to the position my son took that morning as I dropped him off at school: the difference between right and wrong is merely an opinion. As a high school kid, my son probably didn't know the word "postmodernism." But you don't need to know the label and its history to recognize the thought process. It's what moral philosopher James C. Edwards calls "normal nihilism."

"To be a normal nihilist," Edwards explains, "is just to acknowledge that, however fervent and essential one's commitment to a particular set of values, that's all one ever has: a commitment to a particular set of values."[1]

Edwards contends that our choices of moral values—our essential beliefs about right and wrong—are philosophically indistinguishable from our taste in coffee. You like a cinnamon dolce latte coconut half-caf with whipped cream. I drink my coffee black. We differ. Ultimately, he contends, we choose our values just as we order a cup of coffee, or choose how to dress, or decide what music to listen to, or how to furnish our living spaces. As Hans Küng, the Dalai Lama, and the Parliament of the World's Religions have all argued, secular humanists and religious traditions globally agree on certain universal moral values—do not lie, steal, kill, or commit

---

1. Edwards, *The Plain Sense of Things*, 47.

sexual harm.² But Edwards has a point nonetheless: we are apt to disagree about how these universal moral norms are to be applied in particular circumstances.

For instance, is it "theft" when CEOs earn fabulously more money than workers? Are same-sex unions "sexual harm"? What about capital punishment and government torture? Do they violate "do not kill" as a universal moral norm? What about tax subsidies allowing the working poor to purchase health insurance? I think that the poor should not be allowed to suffer or die from treatable diseases simply because they can't afford to see a doctor: I see health care as a human right, and furthermore a vital foundation both for public health policy and for the common good. Others regard regular access to health care as a consumer good: it's appropriately accessible only to those who can afford it. They don't see why they should be taxed to pay for insurance covering some stranger's chemotherapy. We differ.

And that's Edwards's point: in the end, our moral commitments are philosophically indistinguishable from our lifestyle choices. Even if we were to argue about single-payer national healthcare plans until the cows came home, we would never resolve our differences. All we could achieve is tracing our different positions back to different initial assumptions and definitions. Every intellectual position is based upon initial assumptions and definitions. These initial assumptions and definitions differ.

Or at least they *can* differ. When these differences cannot be reconciled, or when the people arguing cannot agree upon some third set of initial assumptions and definitions, stalemate ensues. There is no getting around the need for initial assumptions: we *do* pick our starting points, whether consciously or unconsciously, whether deliberately or by assimilation from our own cultural location. That's what my son said that morning: all this right and wrong stuff is just an opinion. It has no solid intellectual basis from which one can reason rigorously and objectively about morality. Moral claims all descend from assumptions, presuppositions, and definitions that are not writ in stone. And if they are not writ in stone, if

---

2. Küng and Kuschel, *A Global Ethic*; Dalai Lama, *Toward a True Kinship of Faiths* and *Beyond Religion*.

they are not absolute and beyond all reasonable question, then they are, in the end, arbitrarily chosen. There is no middle ground.

Or so the argument goes.

Morality as A "Choice"

What Edwards argues is similar to what Kierkegaard argued in the early 1800s: morality is a choice people make. For Kierkegaard, there's a heroism involved in any commitment to a given moral system such as Christianity. There's grandeur in deciding to be honest or compassionate despite the absence of rigorous intellectual proof that honesty or compassion are the absolute and beyond-all-question correct moral values. There is moral grandeur in recognizing both our capacity for horrific cruelty and our capacity for heart-stopping generosity—and then choosing to go with generosity, despite the disadvantages that the generous may suffer in a world filled with cruel and rapacious individuals. But perhaps there's nothing grand about it at all: perhaps morality is something like a consumer choice, like deciding how to dress or what style of furniture to buy. Perhaps claiming moral grandeur in arbitrary opinion is simply grandiose.

Is that really the case? If there is an element of *choice* in moral decision-making—if it's not all absolute obedience to absolute authority—does that make the choice trivial? *Merely* personal opinion, like my preference for Birkenstocks or Merrells rather than three-inch power heels? Really? That seems improbable. That feels as wrongheaded as authoritarian absolutism. Morality need not be as exact as the calculus in order to function successfully in a culture.

But here we are: this is the impossible predicament we see all around us all the time. On the hard Right, there is the public image of Christianity, which in the eyes of many is dominated by an abusive judgmentalism that tries to silence all debate and coerce all of us into conformity. On the equally radical hard Left, there is normal nihilism, which is in its own way no less silencing and no less coercive. I've seen disagreements about moral issues skid to a halt repeatedly when someone protests, as someone always does, "but each person has to decide for herself what's right and what's wrong!" The objection serves as a warning flag, as a traffic sign cautioning that a bridge is out: don't go there; danger ahead. Someone adeptly changes the subject; the conversation skids into a turn. I sit back, feeling the anxiety in the room. That's Edwards's normal nihilism at work.

When that happens, I always want to argue back. I don't, I confess. I don't want to corner my friends as I cornered my son that day. I don't want to be rude. But I *am* curious, and so I'd like to pursue here the questions I don't ask my friends.

Personal Opinion?

Questions like this: Are moral norms really a matter of personal opinion? Do you mean that? If it's up to the individual to decide what's right and what's wrong, then what about the sincere pedophile? Pedophiles commonly insist that they are not harming children. Does that mean their behavior is acceptable? Most suicide bombers are probably convinced that what they are doing is right. Does that make it right?

The same issue shows up in less violent contexts. Every politician accused of corruption, like every Wall Street financier accused of fraud, stands up and says, "I did nothing wrong." They are not usually contesting the facts. They are claiming that what they did wasn't "wrong." If they thought it was morally acceptable—if their lawyer found a loophole—does that mean they did nothing wrong?

Or what about bloggers, politicians, and telecasters who knowingly and repeatedly make false claims? Are they are trying in various ways to profit from the well-known psychological fact that many people will come to believe any lie that they have heard repeated often enough? Is that "wrong"? Or am I being picky here? Am I confusing mere "infotainment" with morally serious political discourse? Is infotainment located in some reality-free realm where truth doesn't matter and it's inappropriate to expect responsibility to the facts? Who's to say? *How do you know?*

Despite appearances, despite the casual ways in which friends try to avoid argument during dinner, no one seriously believes that we can reduce the difference between good and evil to merely personal opinion. That's not the issue here, not for my son, nor my friends, nor even, I suspect, for James C. Edwards.

The real problem is this: many of us are deeply suspicious of religious absolutes. The difference between good and evil is far too important, and real life is far too complicated, to defer mindlessly to rigid religious authority. Religious authorities have too often shown themselves to be narrow-minded, corrupt, and self-serving. Most of us worry far more about the dangers of absolutist fundamentalism than we do about what Edwards calls the "normal nihilism" of the extreme Left, if only because in the end we trust that good people will in fact have "good opinions."

But unless we are very careful, our distrust of moral absolutes can trap us in an equally unworkable rhetoric of "personal opinion": make up your own mind about what's right and what's wrong—but don't trust yourself either. When questioned, shrug; when certain topics come up, wave that "bridge closed" warning flag. It's all up to anybody. *Whatever.* Who knows what's right? I have my opinions, but I'm reluctant to stand up for what I think. It's just what I think. Or maybe, more dangerously yet, *I haven't a clue where I stand so I don't want to talk about moral issues at all.*

That's normal nihilism. It permeates our thinking. In *True to Life: Why Truth Matters* (2005), philosopher Michael Lynch adeptly demonstrates that we do care about the difference between truth and falsehood. We care because we are (reasonably enough) convinced that knowing the truth is, all things considered, much better than not knowing the truth. For instance, knowing what's true is necessary for our ability to achieve the good that we seek in life. We will never know absolute truth absolutely, he admits. But we do have public standards of clear logic and public standards for the handling of evidence.

Like so much else in our heritage from classical antiquity, these standards were reclaimed by the scholarly efforts of the first Christian humanists. As any educated person today knows, serious thinkers support their claims with evidence, with logical analyses of evidence, and with lines of reasoning explaining how this evidence supports the claim they are trying to advance. Serious thinkers are by definition open to contrary evidence and contrary reasoning in support of different claims on the same issue. Solidly based argument among such thinkers does not provide "absolute" truth, but it does offer a major alternative to the merely personal opinion of normal nihilism.

Despite the cultural prominence of these ancient, reasonable standards of critical inquiry and responsible discourse, we get hung up on questions of moral judgment because—as I have seen in my friends—we don't want to be judgmental or moralistic. As a result of that diffidence or moral uncertainty, the judgmentalism of the political Right is commonly mirrored by the "tolerance" of normal nihilism on the Left. As Lynch explains, classic liberalism all too often lacks workable terms in which to lay claim to responsible moral judgment, especially moral judgment in political affairs:

> ... liberalism involves equal respect for different conceptions of how to live. The ultimate way of showing respect is to say that every view of the good life is equally true. ...This is bad news. From the liberal perspective, its most tragic flaw would be that it is self-defeating as a political position. As I noted, the liberal must herself acknowledge that, in advocating liberalism, she is advocating one view among others of the good life. But if it is part of the liberal's view that every view of the good life must be seen as equally true as her own... then it is unclear why she is advocating liberalism at all. If her opponents' views—those, say, of the fundamentalist Right—are equally true as the liberal's own, then what motivation does she have for opposing them?... I think you'll recognize this view—call it *relativistic liberalism*—as a fairly common one. As a result of its influence, it is not surprising that defenses of liberal causes have become so mealymouthed and weak in recent years. It is hard to stand up and fight for a position that by definition takes itself to be no better than any other on offer.[3]

What Christian humanist progressives have to offer, then, is a defense that is neither mealymouthed nor judgmental and moralistic. We have a vision of radical hospitality based upon (a) compassionate

---

3. Lynch, *True to Life*, 164–65.

reverence for the image of God in everyone, (b) moral obligation to the common good, and (c) particular concern for the marginalized, who so commonly lack full access to the common good. We also believe that (d) critical intelligence and rigorous argument are the light of God within us. We reflect that light only imperfectly, and so we must collaborate. But (e) we are morally obligated to think just as we are morally obligated to care.

I contend that this radical hospitality offers a direct and potent antidote to the dysfunctional complexity of shame, bullying, and judgmentalism in American culture. There are other antidotes from others traditions: I wouldn't deny that for a minute. (For instance, Tara Brach offers a brilliant Buddhist antidote to shame in *Radical Acceptance* [2003]; Pema Chödrön offers another Buddhist approach in her retreat recording, *Getting Unstuck* [2005].) Wise advice from other traditions does not threaten my belief that what Christian humanism offers is both remarkably valuable and richly *humane*.

In the absence of an outspoken Christian humanism, American culture as a whole would far too easily divide between what Lynch calls the "mealymouthed" diffidence of liberal normal nihilism on the hard Left and the judgmentalist condemnations of Christian fundamentalists on the hard Right. And if the only choice is between nihilism and judgmentalism, then good people who believe in truth and who honestly seek the good in their lives may be tempted to opt for religious judgmentalism instead. Good people horrified by nihilism can be seduced by claims that judgmental fundamentalism is the only alternative to moral chaos and the destruction of the common good.

Humanism properly understood in its rich fourteenth-century origins provides an alternative the equally unworkable extremes of moralistic judgmentalism and normal nihilism. This alternative is becoming increasingly prominent culturally, although until now there has been no clear name for it that bridges the secular-religious divide. I call it *humanism:* Christian humanism, secular humanism, spiritual humanism, Jewish humanism, Buddhist humanism, Muslim humanism, Hindu humanism, and so forth. We believe in the *humane* as a set of moral standards; we believe in *critical inquiry* as a set of intellectual standards that can get us to reasonable probabilities and good approximations and workable compromise positions on honestly contested issues. That's a big improvement on polarized stalemate.

In the aftermath of Europe's great religious wars, European intellectuals were determined to find an alternative to rigidly dogmatic religious judgmentalism, because they had seen firsthand the spectacular political violence that such judgmentalism can evoke. They were convinced that this search would succeed because they were persuaded by Christian humanism and by other, even more ancient sources that critical intelligence is the light of God shining through each of us. Their success—and their failure—delineate the challenge we face today in confronting Christian religious judgmentalism.

8

The Great Enlightenment Project

By 1660, after more than a century of devastating violence, Europe's religious wars had finally burned out, just as what's happening in the Middle East today will someday burn itself out. But in 1660, no one knew that the bloodshed had ended. No one could remember a time when Christians were not at one another's throats. Morally sensitive critical thinkers of the day faced a peculiar and culturally unprecedented question: if morality is not based on ancient religious texts and teachings, upon what *is* it based?

For more than a thousand years, Christianity had provided the conceptual foundation for how people in the West reasoned about right and wrong and why they could feel confident about the validity of their conclusions. But that foundation was no longer structurally sound: "the" church had now exploded into dozens of competing sects. Central Europe lay in ruins, its major cities destroyed. There were now profound—indeed murderous—disputes about sacred texts, sacred liturgies, major doctrines, appropriate church organization, and so forth. The old consensus was gone forever. Or if not exactly *gone*, disputes among Christian sects had become such a devastating source of violent conflict that many people distrusted "organized religion" altogether. As I said before, as scholars by the dozen have explained repeatedly, Enlightenment thinkers did not reject religion. They rejected its abuse and exploitation for political

THE GREAT ENLIGHTENMENT PROJECT

purposes. They did so because they had seen the violence such abuse unleashed, just as we have seen it in our own day.

And so there was a radical need to rebuild a consistent intellectual foundation for the social order—for politically and legally necessary concepts of right and wrong. What would replace "the" church and its powerful leaders? Philosophy stepped up, proposing to derive morality from secular and self-evident truths rather than from sacred Scripture or church teachings. That has come to be called "the great Enlightenment project."

No one doubted that the project would succeed because the basic outline of morality seemed self-evident. The argument went something like this: If it's possible to base our public moral norms on self-evident premises—on reasonable claims that all clear-minded people can agree upon universally—then we can escape the threat of theocracy. We can call a halt to superstitious irrationality in any form. We can stop "religious" leaders who are preying upon the piety and the fears of the naïve multitudes in order to seize power for themselves.

Imagine, if you will, the potent appeal of an objective alternative to sharia law that might be honestly and equally acceptable to Sunni, to Shi'a, and to secularists across the Middle East. That was the Enlightenment project in Europe in the 1600s and 1700s. That's what they were trying to come up with—and why they were desperate to succeed. These exhausted survivors agreed about one thing: *keep these doctrinal disputes out of politics.* Dogma cannot be an excuse for killing people, no matter what you think "your God" commands.

I came of age convinced that the Enlightenment project simply had to succeed. When I went off to college in August of 1968, it was as passionately clear to me as it was to anyone in the 1600s or 1700s that morality had to have a logically solid, self-evident, non-dogmatic foundation. Morality had to be derived intellectually, not from the unquestionable authority of church authorities, whether Protestant or Catholic. Those men were not to be trusted. Power corrupts, absolute power corrupts absolutely, and "the church" was far too often corrupt. It seemed to me that the higher a man was placed within "organized religion," the more likely it was that he'd be unapologetically racist, sexist, absolutist, and vehemently "law and order," working furiously to silence Christian political progressives (along with the academic biblical scholars and historians who dared to support them). I stopped going to church. I carried back to my dorm room several of the likeliest volumes of the Copleston anthologies of philosophy. There simply had to be some reasonable, systematic way to explain what we are doing when we are thinking accurately and precisely about the world around us. Obviously we are capable of such rigor and precision: look at our technology. How do we do that? What would that same critical intelligence show us if we used it to ask moral questions?

I wasn't sure what the intellectual foundations of morality might be, but I thought surely someone knew. Someone had to know. I'd find my way to such thinkers sooner or later if I kept reading. So I kept reading.

The philosophers I began reading asked all the right questions. They wrote and thought with a verbal precision I found nearly intoxicating. They had the questions, the questions my date and I had struggled with on the night of the Kent State shootings even as the last piece of pizza grew cold and the waitstaff began setting chairs upside-down upon the tables. These philosophers could think with a clarity I had never before encountered. I could not imagine that they would fail to find the answers they sought to questions like these: What is "knowledge"? What is "truth"? And ultimately, "Who or what can be trusted? And why?" *How do you know?*, that question that tasted like a nightmare of acrid smoke and terrified screams.

But they did fail. The great Enlightenment project failed. We are the heirs of that failure. That failure is visible in our impossible predicament, which is the unworkable choice between the radical individualism of normal nihilism on the hard Left and the abusive judgmentalism of the hard Right. The story of the Enlightenment project failure needs to be told, because bits and pieces of this heritage still wash up on the shore of our common cultural consciousness. In our efforts to confront and refute fundamentalism, we pick up and carry home parts of arguments without necessarily understanding the larger whole from which these particular convictions have come loose.

Kant and the Need for Moral Autonomy

In the later 1700s, Immanuel Kant argued—at great length, and with eye-crossing complexity—that we must be morally autonomous. That is, the moral law must come from within us, not exclusively nor arbitrarily from God nor from contested interpretations of ancient manuscripts. If moral law comes only from outside of us, Kant explained, then we are not morally free. But if we are not morally free, then neither are we morally responsible. To be responsible, to be accountable, we have to have a real choice in how we behave. We have to have "free will."

This is the claim I still hear my friends making in their objections to religious judgmentalism: it's up to each person to decide what's right and what's wrong. We have to figure this out for ourselves.

That's like being told *invent the wheel* (and the axle, the ball bearing, and the cotter pin). Invent the calculus. Build your own phone and all of its apps. Morality is a do-it-yourself project: you are on your own here. There is no owner's guide to being human, no help screen, and customer reviews are a field of flamethrowers.

But "figuring it out for ourselves" on an issue-by-issue basis is not what Kant meant. What Kant meant is that moral norms have to be logically derived from a starting point that each of us can accept for ourselves or apply to our own lives without any loss of moral freedom. In a quite paradoxical way, then, Kant belongs to the "look outside yourself" moral tradition: *look outside yourself* to the most rigorous standards of logic. *Look outside yourself* to self-evident philosophical premises whose "self-evident" status reflects Western philosophical tradition at its most rigorous (and most Platonic).

Because we are all inherently and identically logical thinkers, Kant assumed, if we proceed in this way, then we will agree *and* our agreement will be "free." Rigorous philosophical logic, he assumed, transcends cultural context. Its truths are absolute, just as "$2 + 2 = 4$" is true regardless of cultural context and social location. That was an assumption shared by almost everyone in his day.

Moral Norms and Free Will

The important point here, Kant's point, is that moral norms depend upon free will. That is, for an act to have moral weight or moral significance, the person involved must have the essential freedom to do or to think otherwise.

Let's stop for some examples. For instance: If I think 3 × 7 = 10, I am making a mistake. But if the facts are laid out for me clearly enough, I will change my mind. I will see why 3 × 7 = 21; I will agree *freely*. That's the clarity Kant sought for moral norms: there has to be some line of reasoning that convinces me of moral norms, just as a good math teacher might convince me of the truth of the multiplication tables.

Here's a more difficult example: If I report my income honestly to the IRS simply because I'm afraid of getting caught, I still count as a law-abiding citizen. IRS auditors do not care about my motives. But my motives *do* matter for the moral significance of my income tax return. For my tax return to have moral significance, I have to be reporting my income and deductions honestly because I am freely convinced that's the morally right thing to do. My motive does matter. In Kant's terms, I have to be paying my full share of taxes because I am authentically or personally motivated to do so, not simply because I'm afraid of being audited.

Similarly, there's a difference between obeying the ten commandments simply because tradition says they were given directly by God himself however many years ago, and obeying the ten commandments freely. For instance, I might obey the Ten Commandments freely because I believe they offer guidelines for a life that is honest, authentic, grounded, mature, decent, and so forth. But if I obey simply because I'm terrified of eternal torment by a vindictive God, that's something else again. My behavior—however admirable it might seem to an outside observer—has been coerced. It is not morally free, and so it's not morally significant either.

Theological sidebar: Are the Ten Commandments true and reliable guides to a humane life *because at some specific historical moment* they were given to us by God? Maybe it's this instead: Ancient stories attribute these teachings directly to God himself in a fabulously dramatic scene within a compelling story of people fleeing across the desert because that's how that culture taught, preserved, and proclaimed its wisdom about how to lead an humane life. Such wisdom was deeply rooted in their spiritual experience—in their inward perception of divine Presence—but that's not to say that God himself wrote the Commandments on stone tablets at some particular historical moment. Like the Buddhist Six Perfections or Ten Perfections or Eightfold Path, the Ten Commandments are a summary statement of the spiritual wisdom of a great tradition—in this case, a tradition that entrusted its wisdom to the world-class power of its storytellers.

Moral Autonomy and Fundamentalism

Radically authoritarian Christians would be horrified by the possibility that I might decide *for myself* that the commandments are true, as if I have moral standing somehow to decide for myself whether murder is immoral, or theft is, or adultery. But that's not exactly what I'm saying. I'm not saying that I decide for myself whether murder is morally acceptable. I'm saying that I have to see for myself the validity of the thinking behind the commandment "thou shalt not kill" or "thou shalt not commit adultery."

By comparison, there's a difference between accepting the periodic table of elements on the basis of deference to authority and understanding for ourselves the truly breathtaking elegance of the chemistry or chemical analyses reflected in how that table is arranged. Those of us consciously or unconsciously influenced by Kant and Kantian tradition feel that *of course* we have to see for ourselves and be intellectually satisfied that certain key moral claims are valid. But that is, I admit, an assumption that these moral claims are based on rigorous logic and the facts of human social experience rather than exclusively upon the revealed will of God (or, by analogy, either the chemistry teacher or the chemistry textbook). Fundamentalism insists that faith is based on deference to the utterly unquestionable authority of God as mediated to us by an infallible pope or by an inerrant book.

Despite fundamentalist horror at my scandalous presumption that I should *see for myself* that "the Word of God" is true, Christian teachings for centuries have included long thoughtful commentaries on the ten commandments or on the Sermon on the Mount, one of Jesus' major moral teachings. Such commentaries endeavor to elicit this deeper, intellectually more sophisticated assent of the morally free will. And in parallel fashion, good chemistry teachers do not say "because I say so" or "because the book says so." Even in high school chemistry courses, good teachers explicate the physical logic of the periodic table.

The free assent of the free will is necessary to establish the moral status of a behavior just as the free assent of a free people is necessary to establish the legitimacy of a government. Without this free assent of the free will, all we have is obedience. Conformity. Mere obedience to religious requirements, more or less mindless conformity. Mere obedience might be coerced from a slave—or somebody threatened with a billions of years of excruciating torture in the afterlife. Such obedience is not the free conformity of the free will to moral truth. There is no spiritual transformation or spiritual maturing involved. And—my larger point here—a religion rooted in mindless conformity is asking to be co-opted by those seeking political power and social authority for themselves.

The point I'm arguing here may seem obvious. But it's not obvious at all. Or if it seems obvious, that's a measure of Kant's monumental influence upon the moral thinking of people who have never read a word the man wrote. The position I'm taking—Kant's position—is deeply controversial. It is appallingly, heretically, profoundly immoral among those Christians for whom morality consists in our abject and absolute obedience to (what someone has told them is) the will of God.

Nonetheless, an equally substantial tradition within Christian moral theology would insist that coerced obedience does not engender spiritual transformation. Compelled obedience doesn't give a life meaning. It doesn't provide anything of genuine moral substance to the choices a person makes. But there is real substance to the spiritual quest for moral truth. There is transformative power in the personal quest for the wherewithal to live in accord with the spiritual truths one has discerned. For instance, and as I have argued at length in *For Fidelity* (1998), sexual fidelity as a highly intentional choice does make an enduring contribution to any marriage.

Coerced obedience has its uses, of course: the force of law provides a necessary level of social order. If more people were more consistently law-abiding, the world would be a much better place than it is. Handgun violence. Hedge-fund malfeasance. The abuse of children. If nothing else, there would be fewer accidents if everyone drove at the speed limit and stopped promptly at stoplights. Moral autonomy may be invaluable, but we still need traffic cops, IRS auditors, people screening carry-on bags in airports, and effective regulations.

But God does not coerce. God invites. God offers help in diminishing certain avoidable aspects of human suffering, which is (in the Christian humanist vision) the suffering that we inflict upon one another. We have minimal control over diseases and natural disasters. But we can do something about the ways in which "man is wolf to man"—*homo homini lupus,* which may in fact be a slander upon the character of wolves.

The Problem with Moral Autonomy

Our legitimate need for social order is not the issue here. The question at hand is logically prior to keeping order. The question is this: what is the foundation of morality if we are not going to accept the unquestionable and infallible truth of ancient religious Scriptures and religious institutions? Why is "moral autonomy" something other than an invitation to egregious immorality such as pedophilia, sex trafficking, or suicide bombing of civilians?

Kant's foundation for morality was to derive morality logically, step by step, from a major claim that the free will can freely accept as both morally true and personally applicable (by analogy, that's like seeing the logic behind the periodic table). Kant's nominee for this major claim goes like this: we should all behave in such a way that we could wish our behavior would be a universal law for everyone everywhere. That's his categorical imperative.

When I was first struggling through Kant, that struck me as an unduly labored, roundabout way of formulating the familiar Golden Rule. It sounded a lot like what my parents used to say: *what if everybody did that?* (Chagrined, I'd pick up the candy wrapper I had dropped, or I'd stop picking at the spot where the varnish had chipped on the church pew.) I thought Kant's categorical imperative worked pretty well.

Unfortunately, it doesn't work. And here's why it doesn't work. Turning my behavior into a law for everyone's behavior across the board means turning my preferences into a law dictating everyone's preferences. That only works if all people everywhere think as I do, value what I value as I value it, live in the same subculture I live in, and face the exact same kinds of moral conflicts that I face.

For instance, what if I neither want nor need government subsidies to help me afford health insurance? Why then should I pay taxes to help others who do need those subsidies? A sharp Kantian who knew public healthcare as an issue would of course have multiple comebacks to persuade me to change my mind. Nonetheless, Kant does assume a pre-existing similarity of moral conscience. He could do so coherently because his world was both monoculturally Judeo-Christian and complacently ethnocentric. The categorical imperative works best when every adult conscience has already matured within or internalized the same wide array of moral and social norms, such that the task of philosophy is simply to demonstrate on abstract grounds what these norms are and why they are valid. What might look to us like ethnocentricity was understandable in an elite male scholar in Prussia in the 1700s. But it's problematic now. Now we are living in a much bigger conceptual universe.

In saying that, I do not deny that there are transcultural moral norms: do not lie, steal, murder, or commit sexual harm. Nor do I deny that these transcultural moral norms are probably rooted in evolutionary pressure among social obligates to behave in prosocial ways. But as I said before, the devil is in the details: we can disagree sharply over how these lofty principles apply to particularly complicated or ambiguous situations. Being human, being *humane,* is never a simple affair. Philosophy at its best, like religion at its best, is an honest guide to that complexity. The question at hand here is whether or not Kant's philosophy provides the philosophical equivalent of a "proof of God." Does it provide an *absolute*, a universal truth, from which morality can be derived as a closed logical system dictating the difference between good and evil actions?

And it doesn't. And there are no "proofs of God" either. Was Kant even *trying* to construct such a closed system? I'm not sure. Centuries later, we are far more suspicious of closed systems than anyone was in the 1700s. In the 1700s, people were far more likely to assume that morality as defined by Christianity was in fact logically self-evident to any unbiased observer.

There were, of course, alternatives to Kantianism. Let's look at one: David Hume.

9

David Hume's Alternative: The Good Heart

David Hume, a Scottish philosopher a generation older than Kant, offered a different approach to secular morality. He is often paired with and contrasted to Kant, who was deeply influenced by his work. Hume's approach is very different: he clearly belongs to the "look within yourself" school of ethical theories. For an American sensibility, British empiricists like Hume will always feel much more down to earth and accessible than Continental rationalists in the difficult, abstrusely technical tradition to which Kant belongs.

In the 1740s and 1750s, Hume argued that we can't possibly base morality upon mere rationality: logical thinking does not dictate human behavior. Our logical arguments or commitments are far more likely to *follow* our passions rather than lead them—what Jonathan Haidt in *The Happiness Hypothesis* (2006) has more recently described as the rationalist rider on the mighty elephant. What matters for morality, then, is having good heart (or a moral elephant). Moral behavior does not derive from the intellectual ability to perform a swift and consistent deduction from some self-evident first premise. That's not how the mind works, Hume insisted—although philosophers since Socrates had often portrayed morality as functioning in exactly this way, as a rigorously intellectual process that is innate to the moral character. Hume contended that such rationalism is a wildly inaccurate account of actual human behavior. And of course a fair amount of recent neuroscience now agrees with Hume's critique of strict rationalism.

Hume argued that morality derives from our gut feelings of approval and disapproval regarding actions that are either useful or pleasant to ourselves and to others. Like Kant, Hume makes a convincing philosophical case for this position in a step-by-step fashion. It can seem quite persuasive at first. It looks like a rigorous argument that compassion is the basis of all morality, such that, whatever the question, love is the answer. That's appealing. It's also a bit sentimental, or at least it is when compassion is set in opposition to "critical thinking." Compassion minus critical thinking is probably too simple for the moral complexity of life in its most difficult moments.

In the end, Hume's theory is subject to all the same problems we saw with Kant: being "compassionate" does not help us figure out the quandaries we face just as rapid deduction from first premises does not explain how we actually do cope with life's hard questions. In the last analysis, Hume's system works only for people whose good hearts (and critical minds) are already fully mature and deeply situated within the moral beliefs and moral-storytelling traditions of a given culture. And that's why some Christians claim that secular moralities are in fact living on the cultural capital accumulated by rigidly judgmental, strictly dogmatic versions of Christianity: only dogmatic Christianity flatly insists upon and teaches the moral standards that undergird civilization itself (supposedly).

Humean Thought Experiments

Here are some example of the limitations of Hume's approach. Slavery won the approbation of slave owners. Segregation won the approbation of segregationists. Nonviolent protests for civil rights won the condemnation of law-and-order types. The belief that women are the property of men won the approbation of men for thousands of years. In our own day, concepts like "feminist," "liberal," "progressive," "moderate," and "compromise" have become both pejorative terms (in some circles) and central values (in other circles). Furthermore, the contents of these concepts are hotly disputed: does "feminist" mean "male-hating lesbian"? That's what the word came to mean during right-wing campaigns against the Equal Rights Amendment. In short, approbation and disapprobation may reflect little more than existing beliefs, prejudices, and social norms. Who has the most skillful publicist, the most dominant media position, the bigger advertising budget?

The question then arises, where *do* these feelings of approval and disapproval originate? Hume would have answered "human nature." For him, "human nature" was unquestionably and universally defined by the attitudes characteristic of elite, male, European intellectuals. "Human nature" was "how a gentleman behaved and what he valued," circa 1739. What if we recognize that "human nature" is far more various than that? More dangerously yet, what if we recognize that cultural differences profoundly shape "human nature"?

Let me offer some thought experiments here. Consider this: more-or-less arranged marriages remain common among some ethnic groups in America today. What about that? When our kids hit their twenties, and some of their friends moved toward more-or-less arranged marriages, a friend and I took to laughing that this didn't seem like such a bad idea after all. We imagined marrying off our kids to the children of our friends: really now, why not? These matches would be marvelous. The kids would see that in time. We knew—and they didn't—what makes a marriage work, which is congruent values and mutual respect. Surely our sober judgment in these matters was far more reliable than that of hormone-driven late adolescents.

But would we have wanted *our* mothers deciding for us? We stared at one another, suddenly more disconcerted than we wanted to admit. Our parents *had* decided for us: they decided that these were our risks to take, for better or worse. In doing as our parents had done, we were simply agreeing to a different version of "parents know what's best."

Or this: what about parents having a strong say in what their children study in college? Some would say it's negligent—it's a failure of parental responsibility—to allow our children to make lifelong educational choices in the years before their brains are neurologically mature. Some parents who would never arrange a marriage nonetheless supervise every detail of their children's college education and early career choices. As the mother of two English majors, one with a BFA in ceramics as well, I fended off some very nasty remarks from parents—European Americans all—whose children were majoring in business. Some of my more literary friends made snide remarks about my "allowing" our older son to become an engineer. *What would Hume do?* I wondered.

Here's my point: there is no culture-free perspective from which to judge the relative moral responsibility of differently encultured parenting styles. Parents do judge one another—I'm not denying that. I'm simply saying that our judgments are rooted in our own personal and cultural contexts, not in some hands-off, culture-free, morally "objective" truth about "human nature."

"Human" nature? *Humans where and when?* To be human is to be a social creature, a large-brained herd animal with such stunningly flexible behavior that social group norms are massively influential. Whether we approach these differences logically, via Kant, or viscerally, via Hume, we end up in the same predicament: *People take different positions on issues that have obvious and serious moral content. And they can defend the positions they take either logically or emotionally, whichever defense you prefer.* Disputes on such issues all too often dissolve into a shouting match of shabby ridicule, name-calling, carelessness with facts, and flame-thrower rhetoric.

Are There Other Solutions?

In the century or so following both Kant and Hume, other philosophers also tried to derive a universal secular morality from some source other than religious authority. They offered what they hoped were more successful starting points for a philosophically rigorous and hence globally valid moral system. Many undergraduate ethics courses and standard anthologies look at each of these systems in turn, exploring the problems with each.

Consider, for instance, the greatest good for the greatest number. Does that mean we can completely ignore the well-being of the remaining 49 percent the population? What if it's only the well-being of 20 percent? Tell me: at what point am I morally free to ignore the suffering of another human being? For instance: slaves were a majority of the population in the South, but they were not a majority in the nation as a whole, whose economy transparently profited from their forced labor. The greatest good for the greatest number would have left them slaves.

And then, who get to define "greatest good"? *Whatever serves human flourishing* is one standard answer. But who gets to define "flourishing"? And so forth. Even "love your neighbor as yourself" can be deconstructed. How is a valid or healthy version of "self-love" to be defined? By what logic is self-love a universal norm to begin with? Isn't pathological individualism the major dysfunction of Western culture generally?

And on and on it goes, one theory after another.

I've read a lot of this stuff over the years. It gets very depressing very quickly. Plodding through such arguments leaves me restless, needing chocolate, fighting off a nihilist suspicion that morality has no solid basis at all. It seems to be "whatever I think," except that I'm no longer sure what I think. And that diffidence, that hesitance to have any moral position whatsoever, is perhaps the most dangerous predicament of all. It lets me turn my back on far too much suffering and injustice in the world around me. It feels like a dodge for thinking seriously about my own inescapable moral responsibilities—except that I'm no longer sure what my inescapable moral responsibilities actually are. Or if I have any in the first place.

At such moments, the tide of postmodernist uncertainty threatens to swamp my own small boat. I can feel trapped between the cliffs of religionized judgmentalism on the Right and normal nihilism on the Left. Shipwreck feels certain, and all the more certain because I have no idea where I am headed and why. In the absence of a destination—or a destiny—of my own, I'm at the mercy of the currents of popular culture: the latest best seller, the newest YouTube video making the rounds, whatever my own social networks and Google algorithms are telling me. Or advertising and the culture wars, heaven help us all: thousands of claims every week bombarding us from all directions.

It's easy to panic. It's easier yet to ignore all of this because it's disconcerting to think about and perhaps impossible to resolve. As a moral stance, *well, whatever* has its appeal, no doubt about that.

DAVID HUME'S ALTERNATIVE: THE GOOD HEART

Above all, it's easy to understand why people take refuge in authoritative institutions, especially when the local leader is a humane character. Only *some* of us feel morally compelled to think these things through for ourselves, in detail, rigorously and responsibly. Maybe that's a quirky need, or maybe it's neurotic, or maybe it's a curse: but here we are. Some of us feel we have to figure this out.

And so, another analogy: there is no one shoe that will fit every foot everywhere, but from that fact we can't conclude (a) that it doesn't matter what size shoe anyone wears nor (b) that "proper fit" is merely an exalted label for whatever shoe anyone happens to pick out. Over thousands of years of Western civilization, we have learned a few things about moral wisdom just as we have learned a few things about feet, shoes, and gait. Like plenty of other people, I've spent a lot of time and money on orthotics, physical therapy, and gait analysis. I'm neither a runner nor an athlete, but I'm as sensitive as they are to the proper design and fit of a shoe. By analogy, I'm convinced that moral expertise is just as real as any other kind of expertise. I want a workable, nondogmatic, low-controversy, commonsense, culturally sensitive foundation for thinking about morality as the metaphysical equivalent of the properly fitted shoe.

Is that too much to ask? Perhaps. For years I was discouraged and depressed by the fact that my perfectly reasonable desire was so thwarted. But I kept looking. I kept looking because I had to. I kept looking because I was eighteen in 1968 and a sophomore in college in 1970, which is to say I came of age convinced that certain issues cannot be ignored. The next body on the sidewalk might well be mine or my grandchild's, a fact that police violence has brought home to another whole generation.

After decades of this haunted grief (and a lot of quirky reading), I have concluded that *conscience* is a creative process. Understanding that process can provide necessary wisdom to any of us.

⁕

The creativity of conscience will never provide the ironclad certainty that some people find psychologically necessary and other people consider morally necessary. But consider this: what if philosophy had succeeded? Imagine what would follow if philosophy had defined a detailed and logically rigorous morality that was as self-evident as $2 + 2 = 4$? Then what? Then what would you have?

You'd have the secular philosophical equivalent of theocracy, subject to all the same abuses. We saw some of that in the twentieth century. We called it "totalitarianism." The dictatorship of the proletariat, the supremacy of the Aryan race, the unquestionable rightness of whatever theory some elite was using to defend its absolute control over money and power. (The "free market," perhaps. See Harvey Cox's analysis of the free market as a god, and David Graeber's account of the International Monetary Fund. Details are in the bibliography at the end of this volume.) In the end, absolutes are absolutely toxic whether they are religious or secular.

Yes, the Enlightenment project failed. And its cultural heirs spawned the horrors of the twentieth century. And "postmodernism," that slippery term, arose as a broadly based intellectual movement variously demonstrating that absolutes have no clothes.

Absolutes are hazardous, and furthermore they commonly oversimplify complex realities. But that does not mean that moral judgment is an illusion. Nor does it mean that moral judgment is always simply judgmentalism, nor that morality is always moralism. We need to begin again to ask that inescapable question, *How then shall I behave? How then shall I live my life?* and, most painfully, *How do I know?* We need to reach back as far into our cultural heritage as our hands can reach, seeking whatever wisdom might keep the human race alive and flourishing on a healthy planet two or three thousands years from now.

Christian humanism has a lot to offer. What it offers is rooted in its understanding of creativity and its pragmatic appreciation for the reasonable and the probable, not simply the rationalist and the absolutist. As Stephen Toulmin argues in *Return to Reason* (2001), our quest for the rationalist absolute has blinded us to the far older, more modest, more flexible intellectual standard of *reasonable probability*.

10

How Do We Know?

Amidst my own difficult, passionate struggles with the question "how do we know?" I slowly developed for myself a set of tests or challenges that an adequate morality has to pass. Christian humanism meets these standards; Christian fundamentalism does not. Here are the standards:

1. First, the truth-claims of morality cannot depend upon unquestionable dogma or strict philosophical demonstration. The truth-claims of morality must evoke or elicit our consent, not demand it. (The arts can evoke such assent easily: the arts convince, they do not command; the lyric voice clearly says *this is true* without insisting *believe or burn*.) Such evocation might be denied by a reasonable person without self-contradiction, just as the existence of God might be denied by a reasonable person without self-contradiciton. As Kant so wisely understood, moral freedom is required if we are going to be morally accountable. But I've come to feel that conclusive logical demonstration on moral issues is a setup for totalitarian ideologies.

2. Second, a valid account of the difference between right and wrong must be open to the possibility of other, equally valid ways of naming the difference between right and wrong. Kierkegaard has a point: nobody ever has a corner on how most

accurately or most precisely to name (and thus to understand) the spiritual truths from which morality is derived. The truth-claims of morality are much more elusive than that (see point #1).

3. Third, a valid morality must have some way of staying open to new information, new understandings, cultural change, and the facts of changing circumstances. A certain flexibility has to be built in. That's a tall order. But rigid ideologies don't last. They can become oppressive. Or violent. Or at least a source of rigidly polarized political stalemate buttressed by scathing attacks on the moral character and rudimentary intelligence of the opposition. Hume at his best provides that flexibility. A Humean position is systematically open to the networked moral intelligence and the emotional intelligence of people around us. That's wise, because healthy networks trump rigid, ideologically pure hierarchies every time. A healthy network is nimble. A healthy network is capable of recognizing bugs, fixing problems, and issuing updates. Human frailty or imperfection is a fact, not a debilitating source of shame. The "perfect" and the "pure" are relentless enemies of the good. They are also opposed to workable, pragmatic, compromise solutions to complicated problems.

4. Finally, a valid account of the difference between right and wrong has to begin by admitting that every such account is culturally situated. That's the disruptive truth postmodernism brings to the conversation. None of us have access to any personally disinterested, intellectually pure-and-objective point of view. We are culturally located whether we admit that fact or not.

   Cultural contexting is a strength, not a limitation, because each culture has its own wisdom traditions and sources of wisdom. A valid account of morality must provide some access to the accumulated wisdom of its own cultural heritage. Recognizing the wealth and beauty of many cultures does not mean ignoring the particular wealth of a particular culture. Each language has its poetry, but to be a poet or to know a poetic tradition well one must know a particular language in all of its nuances and all of its literary resources. Culturally sophisticated moral insight requires *cultural* literacy. For me, as an American Christian humanist, such literacy has demanded studying both the complicated history and the ancient wisdom of Christianity.

And so, in what follows here, I'll lay out my own best-effort understanding of moral judgment as it is understood within Christian humanist tradition. At its best, I think, this tradition offers a moral judgment that is not judgmental, and a morality that is not moralistic. At its best, Christian humanist tradition meets the tests or challenges I have just laid out.

Or so it seems to me after a lifetime of wrestling with all of this.

The Origins of Morality

If morality is not derived from carved-in-stone "revelation," and it's not derived from the merely personal preferences of normal nihilism, and it can't be derived in any simple straightforward way from "looking around" or from "looking within," then where does it come from? That's the question here. *How do we know?*

Christian humanism as I understand it has an answer: moral obligation follows from the imaginative ability to recognize that the Other or the Stranger is profoundly akin to the self. What we see *looking around* and what we see *looking within* naturally resonate with one another. The inner and the outer paradoxically mirror one another. (Richard Kearney has brilliant things to say about that experience in *Anatheism* [2010].) We are intimates, you and I, whether or not we have ever met. We are together, we are in this together, and to neglect your needs is to neglect my own deep need to be a responsible human being—to be a *mensch*. If I fail to perceive and to honor your humanity, then I warp and dishonor my own humanity. We dwell within a mysterious, inescapable unity with one another that Christian humanism attributes to our unity with God. (If you prefer, you can attribute it to the buddha-nature that we all share, or to the human genome, or to mirror neurons, or to our biological nature as social obligates, or an array of other concepts. Your choice: pick any basis you want for believing that we are born into a profound relatedness with others.)

Or to put it more plainly yet, switching to street-level view: if you want to feel better about yourself, if you want to feel that "we all belong here," if you seek relief from the demons of self-doubt and self-criticism, then you must acknowledge everyone you meet with kindness, empathy, respect, and deference. Look each person in the eye. Look at each person clearly enough and long enough to recognize eye color and shape, openly acknowledging by this small pause that you are a person interacting with another person. If you are interacting with a sales clerk, remember how poorly such people are paid. Be grateful for their competence; admire the dignity of their courtesy. Doing so consistently will change how you see yourself and how you feel about yourself. Not immediately, perhaps. But soon enough. You may be astounded by how many people instantly respond to the recognition you offer. Their faces will light up, more or less brightly, delighted to return to you the small, honest honor you have offered.

I probably learned this from my dad. He often brought me along running errands, beginning when I was eye level with the counter tops—probably when I was four, the winter my brother was born. I wondered what my father was doing that every store clerk brightened so, every hardware store man, every gas station attendant. I thought possibly he was magic. Of course, he was in fact handsome and old-school charming and one of God's original flirts. He had a broad smile, black hair, and sky-blue eyes. Only much later did I realize that he always sought opportunities to acknowledge the people around him. An ordinary working-class guy himself, he never treated others as if they were invisible. That was his faith, I suppose—a concrete practice, not an arcane theory. He had no use for theology at all.

As Jesus says in the Gospel of Luke, "Judge not, and you will not be judged; condemn not, and you will not be condemned; forgive, and you will be forgiven; give, and it will be given to you; good measure, pressed down, shaken together, running over, will be put into your lap. For the measure you give will be the measure you get back"

(Luke: 6:36–38, RSV). We can read such injunctions as references to a control-freak God micromanaging reality to reward the obedient. Or we can see them as psychologically astute spiritual warnings: the only escape from our own self-criticism and self-aversion is through restraining our own judgmentalism. We must overcome our own stinginess of spirit, our own unconscious habits of assuming the worst of everyone, our own fierce unwillingness to cut anyone any slack.

Moral imagination underlies this ability to reframe our relationships with one another. Doing so is a creative act. It's a free, fraught, paradoxical recognition that the different are also and simultaneously the same. There is a pre-existing *relationship* between self and other, a relationship equally dependent upon similarities and differences. And the only way to maintain that relationship is freely to accept the moral obligations it entails to one another's dignity, honor, and well-being.

Moral judgment rooted in this creative act is derived from perceptions and experiences, not from abstract religious absolutes or philosophical absolutes. Neither is it "well-whatever" nihilism: "conscience" is not a grandiose synonym for "my opinion." In Christian humanist tradition as I understand it, morality is existentially prior both to religious dogmas and to philosophical-theological premises, because morality derives immediately from spiritual experience itself (that is, from the experience of self-other resonance, which Christian tradition attributes to compassionate divine Presence dwelling both in self and in other). Morality thus depends upon imaginative cognition. It depends upon the imaginative ability to engage paradoxes and to think symbolically. That's why religious literalism leads so directly into the judgmental fulminations one hears from the politicized Religious Right: they cannot *imagine* their own moral equality with the people they so casually condemn. They can't cope with paradox nor with multiple perspectives simultaneously. Imagination can.

The cognitive power of imagination at work on moral questions shows up as the good conscience. I contend that conscience is rooted in spiritual experience just as painting is rooted in visual experience or music is rooted in aural experience or poetry in linguistic experience. Conscience dwells at the very center of spirituality properly defined.

Within the relevant spiritual experience, there are two key perceptions.

Spiritual Perception #1: The Goodness of All That Is

As I read the tradition, the Christian concept of conscience is based upon two key assumptions. Both assumptions are symbolic perceptions, which is to say both are deeply paradoxical. The first is this: there is a goodness at the very heart of things. Life is good and the world around us is good *despite all the suffering and all the evil that surrounds us*. Despite Ebola and the Black Plague, despite mass murder and sex trafficking, the world is not irremediably evil. The world can be morally good without being perfect, just as we can be morally good without being perfect. Our unwillingness or refusal to acknowledge the good within the imperfect is the "original" moral failure recounted in Genesis.

The claim that the world is good is not an empirical claim based upon excruciatingly precise data sets. It's a moral claim. It's a spiritual perception that there is goodness everywhere just as there is absolutely stunning beauty everywhere, from the tiniest radiolaria deep in the oceans to the most massively billowing nebulae or the most widely arcing spiral arms of a distant galaxy. In the creation account in Genesis, we are told over and over again that "God saw that it was good." The stars are good, the sea is good, the dry land is good, all living things are good, everything is good. Not perfect. Not perfect by any measure. Nonetheless, despite the undeniable reality of pain and death and suffering, at the heart of reality there is goodness. Goodness permeates everything.

But what does that mean? How do I define "goodness"? Like this: at the core of reality we encounter cosmic compassion, because compassion is goodness in action. What "goodness" is, what goodness does, is care compassionately. I once heard Richard Thurman, the great Buddhist scholar, explain that at least some traditions within Buddhism also believe that the essential reality of all realities is compassion. If I understand her correctly, in *Faith* (2002) the eloquent Buddhist teacher Sharon Salzberg says much the same thing: "I was practicing being mindful of my steps, when all of a sudden I encountered what I can only call a tremendous sense of presence, and with it a feeling of release, joy, and love. . . . its essence was this inclusiveness I felt as love; it was big enough to contain whatever sorrow or brokenness might arise. . . . Compassion arose in me, a tender concern for all of us who, within touching distance of such inclusiveness, usually feel so alone."[1]

Christian tradition explains such moments by saying that God is good and the source or the creator of all goodness. Scripture repeatedly defines God as love, as loving-kindness, or as compassion. I'll get back to this point in *Confronting a Controlling God* [forthcoming]. For now, let me say this: by the word "God" I name what I experience as the ultimate or transcendent source of all goodness and all compassion.

That is, when I experience in my own daily life the reality and the power of compassion, I also experience compassion as emanating from some ultimate source that is real. By "real" I mean that whatever this is, it exists outside of me, independently, objectively. But it's so far outside of me that it's beyond my comprehension or ability to define. I cannot establish its objective reality. I can only say that I experience it as objectively real.

That fact frustrates the daylights out of me, I confess, and so if you balk at "God" as an explanation for such moments, I understand. This doesn't make clear intellectual sense to me either. But nowhere is it written that I get to understand everything, nor that what I don't understand therefore does not exist. There's a lot in life I don't understand. Nonetheless, I'll talk about this paradox in greater detail in *Confronting a Controlling God* [forthcoming], chapter 4.

Whatever this is, I call it God. I was taught to call it "God," and that name works for me. I know that there are other names, other names from other people in other traditions. I listen to them attentively because they may understand or see something about what I call "God" that I am not situated to see or to understand. I'm not threatened by such discoveries, because what I call "God" I know

---

1. Salzberg, *Faith*, 120–21.

only *as unknowable*. This paradox is commonplace in Christian tradition. It's exceedingly ancient besides: the contradictory-sounding statement "known *as unknowable*" is a paradox at the center of Jewish spirituality as well. Christians inherit this from the Jews.

The God Known as Unknowable

A God who is known only *as the unknowable* is known or manifest in human consciousness only symbolically, which is to say only paradoxically. That's why ancient Jewish traditions forbade not only images of God but even saying aloud the proper name of God. Many Christian translations of Scripture follow Jewish practice, substituting "God" or "the Lord" as circumlocutions for places where the word in the Hebrew text is "Yhwh."

That's a radical humility. It keeps us turned in the proper direction, which is toward compassionate behavior toward one another and away from inappropriate efforts to define and thus control what cannot be defined or controlled—much less appropriated to our own political and socioeconomic ambitions.

There is no surer sign of the decadent misappropriation of Judeo-Christian tradition than speaking of God with arrogant certainty. The only thing of which I am to be legitimately certain is this: the way of compassion is the only way forward from the suffering, the anxiety, the alienation, and the confusion that surround me at the moment. Similarly, the only way forward from the suffering of the world is the way of compassion. The only way forward from our bloody past is the way of compassion.

The Way taught by Jesus is not a policy prescription. It's a spiritual truth: you must see it *for yourself* because no one can prove it for you or explicate its logic in the ways that arithmetic teachers illustrate multiplication with colored blocks. At most I might elicit your awareness of divine Presence using poetry, storytelling, ritual, music, or architecture. In plain nonfiction prose, all I can say is, "This has been my experience. This is my trust or my commitment to what I have experienced." The Way of compassion has made a difference in my life that nothing else has made. Compassion for myself and for others has been healing.

The Bible records many moments of encounters with the elusive unknowable Presence of the Holy One. These encounters are variously described, depending upon the literary and theological resources available to the storyteller. It seems to me that the single most common literary strategy is *personification*. Elusive and profoundly introspective experiences are externalized as interactions with a figure variously called "God" or "the Lord" or "the angel of the Lord." Sometimes this figure—or perhaps only a voice—appears in a dream, but sometimes this mysterious figure appears directly. Sometimes a figure who at first is identified as "the angel of the Lord" (Judges 6:11) will be described a few verses later as the Lord himself directly present (Judges 6:14). As a literary strategy, this personification allows Hebrew storytellers to externalize and dramatically explore a dimension of human experience that most of us otherwise struggle to see clearly, much less to explain coherently to ourselves or to others. As a strategy within a very long and distinguished storytelling tradition, this personification places spiritual experience at the center of human experience generally. In literary terms, that personification is a bold and fascinating move.

The problem, of course, is that literary personification can be literalized or concretized into anthropomorphism. "God" comes to name a heavenly superhero with magical powers to intervene on our behalf. For more on this, see *Confronting Religious Denial of Science*, chapter 5, "God the Engineer Almighty."

William Wordsworth also wrote about his own encounters with the goodness at the heart of reality. He called such moments "spots of Time." Early in his career he talked about "Nature" and about the quality of his own responses to "Nature." Over time his language became more specifically Christian. But all along he had been allusively linking his own experiences to the text of Scripture. (And—another theological sidebar—Wordsworth's position is not theological pantheism. Nature reveals God, but "God" and "Nature" are not identical. Wordsworth simply encountered God far more easily or predictably in a rural landscape than he did inside a church building. That's true for many people. And it's not automatically "nature worship.")

I think most of us have known a Wordsworthian "spot of Time," whether or not we have called it "God." There are moments in which the world is beautiful, despite all of its pain and all of its problems. Our place in that world is clear: we *belong*, we are *cherished*, although we can't define our place explicitly. We feel that all will be well, although that feeling fails to provide a to-do list, a guarantee, or a set of practical answers to our practical problems. These moments are simply a glimpse of coherence, a glimpse of goodness, a blessed assurance that ultimately somehow everything makes sense. We are beloved. Our place in the world is secure: we belong, we fit in, we have nothing to prove. We are enough, no matter which version of not-enough-ness has haunted us in the past. We are not inadequate in any regard whatsoever: instead we are delighted in. We simply have to keep on keeping on with life.

Enigmatic Spots of Time

These are moments, Wordsworth says, "In which the heavy and the weary weight / Of all this unintelligible world / Is lightened." These experiences are the source, he says, of "... that best portion of a good man's life; / His little, nameless, unremembered acts / Of kindness and of love." And so, he says,

> ... this prayer I make
> Knowing that Nature never did betray
> The heart that loved her; 'tis her privilege,
> Through all the years of this our life, to lead
> From joy to joy: for she can so inform
> The mind that is within us, so impress
> With quietness and beauty, and so feed
> With lofty thoughts, that neither evil tongues
> Rash judgments, nor the sneers of selfish men,
> Nor greetings where no kindness is, nor all
> The dreary intercourse of daily life,
> Shall e'er prevail against us, or disturb

> Our cheerful faith, that all which we behold
> Is full of blessings.[2]

We are of course free to ignore our own "spots of Time." We are free to write them off as transient good moods, or harmonic brain waves, or high levels of certain neurotransmitters. The moments can be explained away easily. Often we do explain them away.

For years, I admit, I brought my own intelligence at its most fierce to explaining away such moments. I explained them away because I wanted nothing whatsoever to do with "the church" as an institution. Although I had been blessed by many fine teachers, I'd had my fill of the institution itself—its abusive authority, its systemic exclusion of women, its acute anxiety about the body. Nonetheless I kept adding to my collection of poems about such experiences. These poems that shimmered on the page like something out of Harry Potter novels. They held up a bright surface in which I recognized what I too had felt, felt but turned away. Good heavens, I'd tell myself, this is not God. This is something else. Creativity at its most powerful, maybe. Imagination at its most powerful. But *God?* Not a chance. "God" belonged to "the church," and I knew all too well what *churches* thought about women like me. *God?* Not a chance.

Over time, that changed. Not easily, not quickly.[3] But eventually I did realize that the churches do not own God. And at this point I can say with scholarly confidence that Christian humanist tradition as I understand it places these "spots of Time" at the very center of imaginative religious consideration. Christian spiritual tradition says that these are momentary encounters with the goodness that dwells at the center of reality itself. And they are, simultaneously, encounters with sacred Presence within us. Such moments are to Christian spirituality what the Big Bang is to astrophysics: here's where it all starts.

2. Wordsworth, "Lines Composed a Few Miles above Tintern Abbey," 34–49, 121–34.

3. And since I'm a writer, of course I wrote a book about that peculiar struggle, a book originally published as *Dance Lessons: Moving to the Rhythm of a Crazy God.* Later it was reissued in paperback and as an e-book under the title *Motherhood in the Balance: Children, Career, Me, and God.* There's a long excerpt posted on my website, CatherineMWallace.com.

And so, that's the first spiritual perception or spiritual experience from which morality is derived and from within which conscience operates as a guide to human behavior: there is a goodness at the heart of everything. In Christian language, this goodness is the Presence or the indwelling of God, who is ultimately unknowable but partially glimpsed or partially encountered as the source of all beauty, all truth, all goodness, all compassion, and all reliably loyal loving-kindness.

Spiritual Perception #2: The Goodness in Us

The goodness of all that is provides only half of the necessary foundation of conscience. There is a second perception. It goes like this. We are good. We good because we are part of "all that is," and "all that is" is ultimately good. As a result of this second perception, we are innately drawn to the good, as if the goodness in us is a magnet, and the goodness around us is a magnet, and the poles of these magnets are always aligned to attract one another. Conscience is our consciousness of that attraction. We are drawn to the good because we are good ourselves.

The same rich paradox applies here that we saw a moment ago: just as the world is good despite the evil and the suffering that are inescapable parts of reality, so also we are good despite our well-attested capacity for inhumanity to one another. Or on a smaller scale, our capacity to be oblivious, to be self-centered, to be screw-ups and jerks and to let people down, even the people we love the most.

Even toddlers demonstrate this preference for the good, according to behaviorist Jerome Kagan. In *Three Seductive Ideas* (1998), he argues on the basis of empirical evidence that toddlers' behavior is guided not by the Freudian pleasure principle but by the desire to see themselves as "ethically worthy." That's true of all of us, he argues. In the Christian account, which is based in turn on an ancient Jewish creation story rather than neuroscience or the behaviorist observation of toddlers, we are drawn to the good because we are part of a creation that is itself morally good. If Christian morality were a branch of classical physics, "the good" would be something like gravity. It is a force (or, more precisely, a relationship) working on all things.

Christian tradition explains that we are drawn to the good for a second reason as well, a uniquely human reason: we are "made in the image of God." To say that we are made "in the image of God" is to make a symbolic claim, not a biological one. Here are the lines in question:

> Then God said, "Let us make man in our image, after our likeness; and let them have dominion over the fish of the sea, and over the birds of the air, and over the cattle, and over all the earth, and over every creeping thing that creeps upon the earth." So God created man in his own image, in the image of God he created him; male and female he created them (Gen 1:26–27, RSV).

The Hebrew word translated here as "image" literally means "picture." It is a pointedly visual word. It's also a wonderful example of Jewish theological wit. What can it possibly mean to say we are the very picture of that which we are expressly forbidden to visualize?

Such daring paradox is a sure literary signal that a writer is speaking symbolically, in the imaginative confidence of a highly developed literary tradition. And that was indeed the case: the creation stories in Genesis were compiled and written down fairly late. The first of several drafts was assembled from oral sources during the 500s BCE during the great "Babylonian captivity" of the Jewish nation, which had been "ethnically cleansed" from its homeland by Nebuchadnezzar. This editorial work at times reveals a sharply contrasting, no doubt intentional set of parallels to the Babylonian creation story, *Enuma Elish*.

Let's stop here for a moment to appreciate this crucial bit of Jewish theological wit. Let's begin with Xenophanes, a Greek philosopher who also lived in the 500s BCE. Xenophanes said that if horses could draw, they would picture God as a horse. But Jewish tradition that says *we cannot picture God* because picturing God or even naming God is a step toward presuming that we know who or what God is. But we don't know, Jewish tradition insisted. We must not pretend otherwise. We encounter the presence of God only as compassion or loving-kindness. The origin of this cosmic compassion is perfectly real, however you want to define "reality," but it is profoundly elusive. It cannot be captured in the nets of intellect, no matter how finely woven. That's why its very name is not to be spoken, and even the name itself is a spectacular conundrum (more on that in *Confronting a Controlling God* [forthcoming], chapters 8 and 9).

In the very same way—by narrative analogy—something at the core of us also remains acutely out of reach to the inquisitive intellect. The human capacity for the good is ultimately as elusive as "God" is. We can neither precisely define nor definitively prove the reality of our own moral capacity. That explains our inability rigorously to define human morality as a self-consistent, rational system. In the ancient poetic language of my own tradition, the most that I can say is this: There is that within each of us which is holy. It deserves all reverence. But whatever this is that both deserves and elicits such reverence, it too is known in only ways that are admittedly and inescapably incomplete. It is defined as beyond definition. Something vitally important about "human nature" is inaccessible to us intellectually but experienced pragmatically and spiritually as our own capacity for moral behavior, a capacity rooted in the deep resonance between self and other.

This symbolic claim about human nature has a single overwhelming implication that goes to the very heart of Christian moral theology as I understand it: we have an ultimate or transcendent moral obligation to the well-being and the dignity of every other person on this planet. No one's life is expendable. Everybody counts; everybody belongs. Or, in the usual theological language, all humans are sacred. We have sacred obligations to one another because God dwells within each of us.

I cannot prove any of this. It's a poetic vision, a religious vision, a *story*. It is reasonable and relatively nondogmatic. That is, many of its key assumptions are accessible within other belief systems or from with various academic disciplines. But as a vision and a story, what I'm saying here is neither self-evident nor demonstrable.

And I'm okay with that.

Immorality and Sin

We are not perfectly good. That's the paradox here. We are not perfectly compassionate with one another. The human capacity for evil is painfully obvious. Here's the point at which we most crucially need imagination.

The primary speech of imagination is metaphor. In one of the major metaphors of the Jewish vision, creation is unfinished. It's up to us to complete it. Or—a second metaphor—creation is dynamic. Creation is growing and developing toward its true nature, and we are called to participate in that growth. Or, in a third equally revered Jewish metaphor, creation is somehow shattered, and we are called to participate in its healing or its rebuilding. We are called to be gifts to one another, not sources of pain. The major Christian metaphor is *food*. The world is starving; we are called to be bread for the world. The world is thirsty; we are called to be the cup of life.

Each metaphor makes a crucial point: we too are unfinished, growing, broken, hungry, thirsty. We are an imperfect part of an imperfect world, called to align the goodness within us (what is *whole* within us, what is *enough* within us) to the best of the goodness and wholeness that is available within any interaction we have with others. Such metaphors have a subtlety and grace that philosophic systematizing cannot match: they are persuasive, pragmatic, and accessible. They are claims made at the down-to-earth, street-level view. They illuminate both the clear mind and the good heart that is in us. They do so first of all by admitting that paradox is inescapable. There is no fruit anywhere that can render us perfect and in control, in clear possession of good and evil.

In the 1200s, in his *Summa Theologica*, Thomas Aquinas argued that Adam and Eve would never have sinned if they truly understood who God was and what a relationship with God promised them.[4] The fact that they did sin, he explains, proves that they did not understand. We never actively choose evil knowing it's evil, Aquinas argued. (Socrates said something roughly similar.) We choose something evil thinking it's good. Or we choose something evil because we think it's the only way to achieve what's good. Or we

---

4. Aquinas, *Summa Theologica* (Ia, 94a:1), 145.

choose something evil thinking that it's better than the alternatives. Or perhaps we feel that we have no choice at all about what to do: our evil actions feel compelled by circumstances around us.

At such moments, our judgment is tragically flawed. Metaphorically speaking, the moral problem is that we are blind or deaf. We are diseased or paralyzed. Or we are starved and desperate. That's why Jesus came among us first and foremost as a healer miraculously feeding thousands. Jesus proclaimed God's universal compassion for all of us; he recalled us to our own authentic, innate compassion for one another. (I have more to say about Jesus's healing miracles in *Confronting Religious Opposition to Science*, chapter 7.)

~

Is what I'm saying heresy? Is this "really" what Christianity teaches or believes? As I've said before, and as I will no doubt say again before long: over thousands of years, "Christianity" has become a very large place. It is an immense conversation, not a set of locked-down absolutes that you must believe or be damned. That said, however, I'm sure that by now some of my readers are starting to wonder, *Is Cate crazy?* That's an honest question. When this book was a lecture series, people asked that question quite pointedly (and with good humor, I might add). What I was saying clashed wildly with the Christianity they had encountered—and commonly rejected—as they were growing up.

Let me try to answer that honest question before I go on to describe in more detail how conscience functions as a creative process. For some Christians, for some *traditions* within Christianity, what I have been saying here certainly is "heresy."

And I'm okay with that too.

11

Is This Heresy?

Depending upon which variety of Christianity you may have encountered in the past, you may resist my two core spiritual perceptions: we are innately good and we are innately drawn to the good. You may resist because, like many people, you have only heard the God of Christianity described as an angry, condemning judge. Given that understanding or that experience, the primary spiritual self-perception is not goodness or beauty but unworthiness, shame, and guilt. We are condemned by God (supposedly) because we are inherently evil creatures who do bad things.

The theological label for that negative self-image is "total depravity." Belief in our total depravity is theologically ancient. And it's a claim worth considering: belief in our total depravity certainly does explain the bloodshed grimly chronicled in the news day after day. Anyone who pays attention to that violence must at times feel that there really is something deeply wrong with human nature.

But is that "wrongness" the whole story? That's the issue here. One major strand of fairly radical Protestantism certainly does see human nature as profoundly and inevitably evil.

"Sinners in the Hands of an Angry God"

In the 1500s, both Martin Luther and John Calvin insisted to their followers that humanity is totally or "innately" depraved. Only a few—the "elect"—will be saved from hell. The elect will be saved not because they are virtuous but because God graciously chooses to exempt then from the damnation they deserve. (As Desiderius Erasmus objected to Martin Luther in the 1520s, such a teaching provides very little motive for anyone to struggle to live virtuously.)

Innate depravity casts a long shadow across all of American Christianity because both the Puritans and the Pilgrims took this theory to heart in central ways. As a result, anxiety about damnation permeated American culture in the 1700s and 1800s. It's clear, for instance, in Nathaniel Hawthorne's fiction. It's equally clear in the archives of personal writing (memoirs, letters, etc.) cogently explored by historian Christine Leigh Heyrman. In *Southern Cross: The Beginnings of the Bible Belt* (1997), she describes the psychological and social consequences of this riveting fear of everlasting damnation and eternal suffering in hell. Such terror was widely evoked by preachers during the Great Awakenings, which were popular religious revivals. These revivals spread across the country in waves in the middle 1700s and again in the middle 1800s.

Consider, for instance, Jonathan Edwards's famous sermon, "Sinners in the Hands of an Angry God" (1741). It's a major text of the first Great Awakening. Although "hellfire and damnation" sermons fell somewhat out of favor after the mid-twentieth century, the God that Edwards describes may nonetheless feel painfully familiar to many people. "God the Condemning Judge" theology can remain in place despite changes in homiletic style. Here's a classic passage:

> The God that holds you over the pit of hell, much as one holds a spider or some loathsome insect over the fire, abhors you, and is dreadfully provoked: His wrath toward you burns like fire; He looks upon you as worthy of nothing else but to be cast into the fire; He is of purer eyes than to bear to have you in His sight; you are ten thousand times more abominable in His eyes than the most hateful venomous serpent is in ours. You have offended Him infinitely more than ever a stubborn rebel did his prince; and yet it is nothing but His hand that holds you from falling into the fire every moment. . . .

IS THIS HERESY?

> O sinner! consider the fearful danger you are in: it is a great furnace of wrath, a wide and bottomless pit, full of the fire of wrath, that you are held over in the hand of that God, whose wrath is proved and incensed as much against you, as against many of the damned in hell. You hang by a slender thread, with the flames of divine wrath flashing about it, and ready at every moment to singe it, and burn it asunder; and you have no interest in any Mediator, and nothing to lay hold of to save yourself, nothing to keep off the flames of wrath, nothing of your own, nothing you ever have done, nothing that you can do, to indulge God to spare you one moment.[1]

If that's who God is, then thanks but no thanks. I want nothing whatsoever to do with such a religion. I'm not interested in a Jesus whose goal in life was intervening between me and such cosmic wrath. I do not believe in a God of cosmic wrath, nor am I willing to worship such a God in an attempt to avoid eternal damnation. But that's not who God is. What Edwards portrays is the God of Charlemagne, not the God of Jesus.

British literary theorist Terry Eagleton suggests that the figure Jonathan Edwards calls divine is in fact demonic. It's the snake in the garden. It's self-berating inner voice of shame and self-aversion. Confusing that figure with the God proclaimed by Jesus is an mistake, a mistake that Eagleton delineates with his usual acerbic wit:

> ... the source of inexhaustibly self-delighting life [whom Jesus] calls his Father is neither judge, patriarch, accuser, nor superego, but lover, friend, fellow-accused, and counsel for the defense. The biblical name for God as judge or accuser is Satan, which literally means 'adversary.' Satan is a way of seeing God as a great big bully. . . . Men and women are called upon to do nothing apart from acknowledging the fact that God is on their side no matter what, in the act of loving assent which is known as faith. In fact, Jesus has very little to say about sin at all, unlike a great many of his censorious followers. His mission is to accept men and women's frailty, not to rub their

---

1. Edwards, "Sinners in the Hands of an Angry God," *The Norton Anthology of American Literature*, volume 1, 252–253.

noses in it. . . . [W]e come to fall morbidly in love with the Law itself, and with the oppressed, unhappy state to which it reduces us, desiring nothing more than to punish ourselves for our guilt even unto death. . . . It is this urge to do away with ourselves as so much waste and garbage to which Freud gives the name of the death drive, the opposite of which is an unconditionally accepting love. . . . The choice is one between a life liberated from this pathological deadlock, which is known to the Gospel as eternal life, and that grisly caricature of eternal life which is the ghastly pseudo-immortality of the death drive. It is a state in which we prevent ourselves from dying for real by clinging desperately to our morbid pleasure in death as a way of affirming that we are alive. . . . This is the hell not of traitors and toasting forks, but of those who are stuck fast in their masochistic delight in the Law."[2]

Terry Eagleton and Jonathan Edwards in effect represent two very different versions of Christianity, each based on a different understanding of God and a different understanding of human nature. This dispute goes very far back in theological history, all the way back to what happened when the very Jewish moral judgment of Jesus ran into the Neoplatonic mind-set of classical antiquity.

Two Views of Human Nature, Two Views of God

Here's the core psychological issue, at least as I see it. Within Christianity, one finds two distinctively different definitions of human nature. In their most moderate forms, these two different definitions offer a variation on the question of whether the glass is half full or half empty. What I described in the last chapter about our innate goodness is the half-full theory of human nature. Let's look at the half-empty theory of human nature.

At its very best, the half-empty theory looks like this: *God loves me despite what a bad person I am. God forgives me; God offers loving support as I try to become the better person God wants me to be.* That line of thinking will have honest appeal to people who feel that

---

2. Eagleton, *Reason, Faith, and Revolution*, 20–21.

they have indeed made serious mistakes in life. In classic Alcoholics Anonymous fashion, perhaps, such faith encourages people to admit their failures and to resolve *with God's help* to become better people. The half-empty theory strongly emphasizes two spiritual truths that I agree with wholeheartedly. First, it is comforting and strengthening to know and to feel that God does not hold the past against us. Second, it is comforting and strengthening to know and to feel that God is always "on our side" as we attempt to amend our ways.

Furthermore, guilt can be appropriate. Guilt can be both psychologically healthy and socially functional. As Philip Reiff argued so cogently in *The Triumph of the Therapeutic* (1966), a culture is heading for very big trouble if "guilt" gets redefined as a psychological symptom to be treated. Guilt can be neurotic and obsessive, of course, but at that point it has become shame, not guilt. But guilt itself—specific remorse for a specific action—can be a mature, healthy response. People incapable of feeling appropriate remorse over their own misdeeds are judged sociopaths.

And so let me say as clearly as possible: the half-empty version of Christianity is nicely attuned to healthy or appropriate remorse. Any reasonable, self-aware person feels remorse on a regular basis. We do screw up. And I think that psychologically healthy versions of this half-empty Christianity are the clear-eyed realists within Christian tradition. We need clear-eyed moral realists because they help us keep our remorse in focus and within bounds. If we lose that focus, remorse can morph into shame. Remorse for specific wrongdoing can explode into the perception that *I am inherently and inescapably defective. I am essentially and irremediably unacceptable.*

But clear-eyed realism needs a solid theological foundation. And at a theological level I flatly disagree with total depravity as a doctrine, even in the moderate form that centers on the belief "God loves me despite my personal and moral inadequacy." I disagree, but not because I buy into the naïve romanticism that insists we are totally perfect just as we are or we are essentially perfectible were the world to stop abusing us.

I disagree with glass-half-empty theologies because God does not see us as inadequate. God does not see us as unworthy. God does not see even the worst among us as a "miserable offender," to pull an old phrase from the 1928 Episcopal *Book of Common Prayer*. God surely sees and understands that our misbehavior causes suffering both to ourselves and to others, but that's not the issue here. The issue at stake is whether God's relationship to us is that of judge to defendant.

Whether or not we are in fact guilty—and in some specific circumstance no doubt we are (or we should be) guilty—God is not properly defined theologically as a *judge*. That is not God's nature. God is not primarily *evaluating* us. That is not God's relationship to us. As Jesus taught, God loves and accepts us; God does not condemn us (see *The Confrontational Wit of Jesus* [forthcoming], chapters 3 and 11).

But you don't have to credit Jesus' authority to reject this image of God as Cosmic Judge. There's another reason. Defining God as the Cosmic Judge is both politically and culturally dangerous because it encourages scapegoating. It encourages a steep divide between us, whom God accepts, and them, whom God rejects. After all, if God is a judge, then God must sometimes reject somebody. A judge who never rejected or condemned anybody would not be a judge.

And that would *never* do. It would especially never do as Christianity and the Roman Empire slowly merged into Western theocracy. In a theocratic system, one of the major functions of religion is providing an ideology that helps the state both to keep order and to legitimate the kind of order that it keeps (see *Confronting Religious Violence*, chapter 3). God-as-Judge theology helps to keep order, with shame (and, if necessary, violence) as the mechanism of social control. Such arrangements are politically quite useful because acute self-aversion can be alleviated by projecting it outward toward the "enemies" of the church-state complex.

And that also explains, I worry, why Christians on the fundamentalist Religious Right offer popular support for government torture, capital punishment, and the aggressive use of American military power, including repeated threats about "all means necessary," which is diplomatic code for the preemptive use of nuclear weapons. And don't forget the political use of incarceration, a scandal described with devastating evidence by Michelle Alexander in *The New Jim Crow* (2012).

Who Can Be Saved?

Within the earliest layers of Christian tradition—in the 200s, say—one finds already formulated a belief that the image of God in us was destroyed by the sin of Adam and Eve in the garden. That loss has been transmitted to us (supposedly, metaphorically) as if through some spiritual equivalent of DNA. Various theological mechanisms were proposed whereby Jesus of Nazareth remedied this loss, such that only through faith in Jesus do we become capable of leading virtuous lives.

As historical theologians by the score have explained, that whole debate reflects Christian adaptation to Neoplatonic influence. The Neoplatonists—unlike the Jews—had a brutally dark view of the human character.

There are dangerous implications to these ancient arguments. The question at stake is whether or not all people everywhere share the same inherent, indelible moral value, the same undeniable goodness that transcendently demands our respect and our reverence. If "the image of God" in us is restored (or its absence remedied) only through some relationship to or faith in Jesus of Nazareth, then clearly it is not restored among non-Christians. Some Christians think it is not (that's one reading of John 14:6). Other Christians regard the universality of God's image within all human beings as beyond question.

That's where I stand. My theological position is bolstered by facts such as this: Hebrew Scripture repeatedly demands "kindness to the stranger"—to the foreigner, the outsider, the immigrant from another culture. In *The Dignity of Difference* (2002), Jonathan Sachs, Chief Rabbi of Great Britain, says that there are thirty-six commands to love the stranger in Hebrew Scripture, but only two to love the neighbor, a claim that Richard Kearney explores at length in *Anatheism* (2010). Loving my own in-group is morally far easier than loving outsiders. But we are quite specifically commanded to love outsiders, just as Jesus loved outsiders. And why? *Because they too are the children of God.*

Let me be clear, of course, that just because the Bible says we are the beloved children of God does not prove in any empirical or intellectually objective way that human nature is inherently prosocial. "What is human nature?" is a question hotly debated in a variety of disciplines: neuroscience, animal ethnology, evolutionary biology and psychology, economics, and so forth. Poets and storytellers have weighed in since time immemorial as well. And in some ways, their answers have been the most influential of all. If I'm told over and over in compelling, creative ways that I am both beloved and capable of great generosity (or worthless and capable of great evil), those messages will influence my self-image and hence my behavior.

Like any other in-house theological dispute, the argument about "total depravity" gets arcanely complicated very quickly. Let me tell one story and be done with it.

Pelagius v. Augustine

A particularly important argument on this issue took place circa 412 CE between Augustine, the powerful bishop of Hippo in North Africa, and Pelagius, a learned monk, said to have come from Ireland but no one knows for sure. Pelagius contended that the image of God in us could not have been destroyed by the sin of Adam and Eve because the human is never powerful enough to destroy the divine. Augustine thought otherwise.

Augustine thought otherwise, I'd argue, because before his midlife conversion to Christianity he was a Manichaean, and furthermore a North African Manichaean. North Africa was home to the most extreme varieties of Neoplatonism and, among Neoplatonisms, Manichaeism ought to win some sort of prize for its essential self-loathing and deep revulsion at human embodiment. Augustine carried with him into Christianity this very dark view of human nature. In Augustine's eyes, we are irrevocably, helplessly broken, a brokenness Jesus came to repair. That's what I was getting at earlier when I talked about a "security liability" in Christian systematic theology: as Jewish Christianity became all-purpose, Roman Empire Gentile Christianity, it became philosophically Greek. Those were the suppositions that Gentiles brought with them from their common culture. As that happened, a quintessentially dark, generically Neoplatonic view of human nature made its way into Christian theological systematics.

That said, it's important to remember that *for his time and place*, Augustine was a moderate, mainline thinker. Given the standards of the day, perhaps that's not saying a whole lot. But it needs to be said, because in Augustine's view our relationship with God allows for God's dramatic transformation of our human character. In becoming one with Christ through grace, an inward spiritual transformation that is enacted externally and ritually in the bread and wine of the worship service, we are restored to a wholeness and to a moral glory that was lost by Adam and Eve. No Manichaean would ever have believed that such restoration was possible. Augustine stands in a tradition that includes figures like Irenaeus of Lyon, who said *gloria dei est vivens homo*—the glory of God is humanity fully alive, or the human fully realized. Irenaeus was not talking about what we mean by "self-realizing." He was talking about our spiritual journey toward inwardly realizing our authentic nature as creatures made in the image of God.

Made *at first* in the image of God, perhaps. But perhaps that the image of God within Adam and Eve was destroyed by their eating the forbidden fruit. Without that inward spark of divine light, Adam and Eve were rightly and appropriately ashamed of their "nakedness."

Pelagius and Augustine argued this point fiercely. Pelagius was steadfast; Augustine was eloquent, prolific, and powerful. My edition of the collected work of Pelagius runs to 350 pages; by comparison, Augustine's collected work is forty-six volumes. Three church councils in a row ruled that Pelagius's point of view was orthodox; a fourth finally sided with Augustine, ruling Pelagius's position heresy.

But by then Pelagius had disappeared from the scene. He had gone back to Ireland, tradition has it; but again no one knows for sure. From the "Augustinian" point of view, the argument I have been making here all along is heretically "Pelagian." (Don't say I didn't warn you.)

In some ways, the dispute between Pelagius and Augustine might seem to be a minor technical dispute over theological trivialities. Why worry about it? Maybe Augustine, situated there in

North Africa, was simply trying to find common ground with the Neoplatonic and Gnostic culture surrounding him. He was adapting the forbidden fruit story to his own locale. But Neoplatonism never made it to Ireland, not by a long shot. And so Pelagius disagreed. He spoke from within a different cultural context, one with a much warmer and more confident view of human nature, and so he interpreted the forbidden fruit story in different ways. Hence the question: a solid 1,600 years later, why worry about this argument between Pelagius and Augustine? Good heavens, Cate, *why bother?*

Here's why. This is the theological "security liability" I mentioned earlier. If we recover some aspect the image of God in us (and thereby escape damnation) only through a theologically proper relationship to God and to Jesus (or to doctrinal claims *about* Jesus) then our immortal fate depends upon being Christian. This leads to the claim *extra ecclesiam nulla salus est*—there is no salvation outside the church, which is the guarantor of theological propriety. *If that's the case,* then there is theological warrant for Christian condemnation of every other religion and, needless to say, the religiously unaffiliated. Only Christians carry the image of God. Everybody else is something less than animals. Animals are at least what God made them to be. Ouch.

But if the image of God is in everyone everywhere no matter what, then what matters is whether we are in touch with and living out the compassionate loving-kindness that is inherently ours. The church might help us in that endeavor, of course. But (a) the church does not have some exclusive franchise rights to salvation and (b) God damns nobody, so what matters here is whether the church does in fact help us to become more compassionate. Does the church help to rescue us from the one-upmanship and from the sense of inadequacy that drives so much of our own negative behavior? That's what the church ought to be doing, and what in many places the church *is* doing—not proclaiming "come to church or go to hell."

In short, I stand in an exceedingly long Christian tradition insisting that *God is in us,* whether or not we go to church. God is in us whether or not we have ever heard about the elusive reality named and not named as "God." It has been said more than once that British tradition is chronically Pelagian. If that's the case (and I suspect that it is), then at its best American cultural tradition is more Pelagian yet: "We hold these truths to be self-evident, that all men are created equal, that they are endowed by their Creator with certain inalienable rights . . . "

Debates about whether "the image of God" survives universally get stickier yet after the Reformation, because (as I said earlier) Augustine's position on this issue was taken up wholeheartedly by Martin Luther and John Calvin. Both of them would also reject the doctrine of conscience that I have just laid out. We cannot be innately and instinctively drawn to the good, they would say, because the image of God in us is long gone. We have no inner moral compass. We still need absolute religious authority to direct our lives. They shifted that absolute, unquestionable authority from its traditional basis in the Roman church hierarchy, relocating it in the Bible. The Bible was to be translated from Latin into local languages; everyone was to be taught to read. That way, everyone could obey the Bible without supervision by Rome.

And yet, in *A Secular Age* (2007), Charles Taylor lays out massive evidence of the controlling, authoritarian turn taken by Christianity under the influence of such ideas. Because we are innately evil, Taylor points out, the "established" Protestant churches happily insisted that state must exert relentless moral control over the population. That's the conceptual origin, for instance, of "dry" cities and counties where it's illegal to sell alcohol. It's behind ongoing alliances between Right-wing evangelicals and Right-wing Roman Catholics to create financial obstacles for women seeking ordinary contraceptives.

In short, even after the Reformation, theocracy continued, albeit now in a slightly new form. That's why the American separation of church and state was so innovative.

In the Image of a God Who Is Love

Let me conclude here by setting out against Jonathan Edwards the following passage from the First Epistle of John:

> My dear friends,
> let us love one another;
> since love is from God
> and everyone who loves is a child of God and knows God.
> Whoever fails to love does not know God,
> because God is love. . . .
> No one has ever seen God,
> but as long as we love each other
> God remains in us
> and his love comes to its perfection in us.
> This is the proof that we remain in him
> and he in us,
> that he has given us a share in his Spirit
>   (1 John 4:7–9, 12–13, NJB).

I once heard a teaching on this passage from Laurence Freeman, the preeminent meditation teacher in the Christian tradition. He pointed out the line "everyone who loves is a child of God"—not everyone who *loves God*, but everyone who loves, period. And if we fail to love, it is because we *don't* know the reality that Christians call "God" (and other traditions, including secular traditions, name in other ways). We are not in touch with this universal source of everlasting, all-inclusive compassion. Something has blinded us to the goodness and to the love that dwell—mysteriously, invisibly, inexplicably—in our own hearts and in the heart of everyone.

That is painful. It causes suffering, first of all for us, and secondly for those with whom we interact. It is nearly impossible, I think, to read Jonathan Edwards without recognizing the acute psychological pain behind his portrait of God's overwhelming wrath toward us.

Christian humanist tradition makes the moral claim that we are all intrinsically good and worthy of love. That's a specifically *theological* claim made by the moral imagination in its Christian form. That is, it's a claim about God and about our relationship to ("made in the image of") God. It's not an empirical claim at all, although there is more or less robust evidence in a variety of disciplines that we are instinctively and biologically prosocial under ordinary circumstances.

Christian humanism is as much a mainstream theological tradition as the harshly judgmental traditions derived (legitimately or not) from Augustine.

It seems to me that what makes Christianity interesting or valuable as a system of thought is precisely this willingness to make a creative spiritual claim that in effect helps to create the reality to which it refers. That is, people are encouraged to see and to act upon their own goodness when you tell them repeatedly that they are good, that they are "enough," that they are welcomed and cherished and their prior failures are not held against them. These beliefs are also enacted liturgically, and a great encounter with the arts can echo in the soul for decades. It can echo for a lifetime. That's why religion matters, or it's part of why religion matters: it's an art. Communal worship is the public performance of that art. And the arts both shape and express how we feel about ourselves and how we feel about one another. In that regard, there's nothing on earth more powerful than the arts.

Seen in this way, Christianity is an effort to change the world. It's not a set of unquestionable doctrines or mean-spirited irrational condemnations of everybody else. It is the practice of radical hospitality. Christianity insists that all of us are beautiful, all of us are cherished, and none of us have anything to prove.

Christianity *does* pass judgment, I suppose. But as a community, our judgment is that many people need a hug and a hot meal. That much at least we can provide. We can't change the world, but we can offer honest welcome and a place at the table.

It seems to me that one of the ways in which Christian humanism tries to welcome and console a suffering world is through our beliefs about conscience. Conscience is the great alternative to judgmentalism. It is a basis for respect, humility, and collaboration. It can provide an intellectually rigorous, spiritually subtle, emotionally satisfying way to fend off shame, inadequacy, and chronically second-guessing ourselves.

So let me explain to you how conscience *works*. Over a lifetime, I have slowly realized that Christian theories of conscience provide what I started out seeking in 1968 after standing on that highway overpass watching smoke rise from riots in Chicago's slums. If in good conscience we disagree about something, as surely we will at times, the process of conscientious discernment prepares us to discuss a contested issue on the basis of logic and evidence, not saved and damned. These debates about logic and evidence will nonetheless be framed by a shared commitment to the common good: we may never be gods, but we can be both morally responsible and reasonable people to work with.

12

Conscience as a Creative Process

Here's my major claim: conscience mediates successfully between the equally unworkable extremes of normal nihilism on the one hand and dogmatic judgmentalism on the other. Conscience can do that because it is a creative process. That is, conscience is or requires the vital operation of the moral imagination.

As I explain in more detail in *Confronting Religious Absolutism*, chapters 10–12, imagination properly defined is the human ability to synthesize patterns. Imagination is the cognitive capacity to "make sense" of experience, beginning with transforming signals from the sensory organs into the perception, "it's snowing outside." The specifically *moral* imagination is also our ability to make sense of our own ethical experience—our own encounters with moral quandaries, our own encounters with the moral and immoral behavior of others. As Samuel Taylor Coleridge famously explained, imagination is the faculty whereby we orient ourselves—consciously or unconsciously—to the compassionate presence that Christians call "God."

In fact, Coleridge argues, the clearest evidence that imagination is a human universal is the fact that we are universally capable of virtue. We are not always and inevitably self-serving. We *do* inherently care about the difference between right and wrong. We care because we spontaneously locate ourselves within patterns of meanings that include the implications of our actions for the well-being of others, upon whose well-being our own also depends. That claim was commonplace in Christian mysticism long before it was also supported by neuroscience, sociology, or epidemiology.

Because imagination is a perceptual process, conscience is a perceptual process as well. Conscience is the faculty whereby we recognize whatever moral good is available within our own situations. Conscience shows up as that "aha!" moment in which we realize what we ought to do, or what we most truly desire if we are to be completely honest with ourselves at some very deep level.

Educating the Conscience

Every perceptual process must be educated. We are not usually aware of that happening for sense perception. (Perhaps we were simply too young to remember.) But we know that a young animal deprived of sounds early on will never learn to hear properly; a young animal deprived of visual stimulation will never learn to see properly. Perception has a learning curve.

What ordinarily happens so effortlessly for sensory perception must happen through deliberate education for more sophisticated kinds of perception. Accountants must learn to read spreadsheets. Orthopedic surgeons learn to read x-rays. English majors learn to read poetry, philosophers learn to read philosophy, architects learn to read blueprints. Entomologists learn to see insects and botanists learn to see plants in precise and detailed ways. Like any other sophisticated perceptual process, the conscience must also be educated. Christian tradition calls that the "formation" of conscience.

This formative educational process has two parts. First, we must do whatever we can to understand the wisdom that our cultural traditions have accumulated. Specifically—and at whatever level life permits—we must study the sages, the poets, and the storytellers ancient and modern, those found in sacred Scriptures and those found elsewhere. We must study the scholars, the mystics and the spiritual masters, the philosophers ancient and modern, and the new evidence on old philosophical questions now provided by the social and physical sciences. We must study the arguments behind the dogma of dogmatists, the creeds of creedalists, and the moral codes (like the Ten Commandments or the Sermon on the Mount) that have been revered for thousands of years. We must study the human experience behind the poetry and the paradoxes of mysticism and other accounts of spiritual experience.

Nobody will ever do all of this, of course. Not a chance. And so no one's conscience is ever fully educated. All of our lives we are always learning. The most outstanding moral teachers in the tradition humbly insist that no one has a corner on truth. In ethics as in any other field of sophisticated inquiry, the best critical thinkers are by definition open to gaining some new perspective on a moral issue. In the meantime, and as I said back in chapter 6, we look around and we ask around as carefully as we can. We listen. We listen most carefully to those who are most different from us, whether that's a difference in age, race, ethnicity, income, gender, or what have you.

For me, as a Christian humanist, all of this study has been constellated around my effort to understand the central religious practice of *radical hospitality*. As I see it, Christianity's heritage of creeds and dogmas don't hold a candle in comparison to the immediate day-to-day practice of radical hospitality. (I'll say more about this in *Confronting a Controlling God* [forthcoming], chapter 5, "Quantum Theology.") Creeds and dogmas, no matter how august, are merely collective experience. They are the opinions and interpretations of others, opinions and interpretations that will reflect their own cultural contexts. Creeds, doctrines, and dogmas are neither philosophical absolutes nor theological absolutes. They are the *wisdom of others*.

We need the wisdom of others. And we are seeking it more widely than ever before. As historian Phyllis Tickle documents in *God-Talk in America* (1997), there was a dramatic rise of book publishing in spirituality and in religion beginning in the 1970s or so. Double-digit growth in book sales testified quite remarkably to how many people were undertaking some of this study firsthand, rather than relying upon the clergy to explain such things. Just as learning a foreign language provided for most of us an entirely new and clearer understanding of English grammar and English sentence structure, so also, for many of us, the thoughtful, sympathetic study of other global religious traditions and philosophical systems has provided remarkable insight into whatever moral system we "grew up speaking."

Whatever the study appropriate to the issues at hand, it must be done carefully and honestly and with non-attachment. The humanist tradition (religious and secular alike) is deeply committed to careful study and to critical thinking as essential elements in the creative process of making hard decisions *in good conscience*.

But study alone is not enough. There is something else we have to do.

Knowing Our Own Lives

To have a well-formed conscience, we must also pay attention to our own lives. Learning how to think critically about our own lives is the second major educational process underlying "good conscience" as a perceptual skill. Within any perplexity we face there are variables that only we can estimate. There are things that only we can see clearly. There are realities that only we are situated to understand. There are consequences only we can foresee, and perhaps only intuitively. Nonetheless, what we know about our own lives is inevitably filtered through what we have experienced in the past. It's filtered through the cultural and social pressures we live with day to day. It's filtered through our own immediate emotional reactions to whatever has happened to us.

As a result, to unearth fully what we know about our own lives, we need friends to whom we can talk openly. We find those friends on our own, one-on-one. We find communities of friends in the book groups and in the support groups that have proliferated so dramatically since the 1970s. We find them at the CrossFit gym, on frisbee teams, in writing groups and book groups, at trivia night at the local microbrewery, at yoga class or the community fine arts studio, and among the parents who sit together on the benches at the local children's museum. Newly facilitated by the Internet, social networks have become dramatically less dependent upon the brick-and-mortar institutions—like churches—that once served as a community's principal locus for social networks.

And yet the brick-and-mortar places still have a role to play, whether that's the gym or the church. Life happens face-to-face. Friendships grow face-to-face. The more we know about nonverbal communication and mirror neurons, the more we understand that life to the fullest doesn't happen online, just as life to the fullest can't be found in books alone. Libraries and Internet searches are marvelous, but they are not enough. Life is much simpler in a library, just as it is simpler online, where Google algorithms direct us to sources that will confirm our presuppositions.

At their best, then, churches can be one of the vitally important face-to-face communities in which we find friends who can challenge our moral assumptions or provide creative new perspectives on the problems we face. Churches at their best, like universities at their best, are intentional communities for education—the education of conscience. Some churches are better at that than other ones, just as some book groups are thought-provoking and some are just an excuse to sit around drinking wine and trading gossip.

In neither situation, however, do I show up wanting to be told what to think.

―❦―

However we get to a good decision—and the paths are many—the decisions we make in good conscience share one key feature. They derive from an imaginative synthesis of the possibilities inherent in our own situation with whatever we have learned about moral wisdom generally. Both elements are necessary. Without the wisdom of the past, we are prey to the blindness of our own era. We lose access to the networked moral intelligence of our own culture and thus to rich support for a mature moral autonomy—for finding those truths we freely accept as both true and relevant to our own situation. But without equal regard for our own insight into our own situations, we can be bullied by a vast array of both secular and religious experts, all of them insisting that they know what's best, some of them seduced by their own will to power. And on top of all that, we can also be deafened by the advice of friends and neighbors and extended family.

The world can feel very full of people eager to tell us what to do. Conscience is our own moral center amidst that din of other voices. But we do need to work at hearing the voice of conscience—that "still, small voice" so easily drowned out by the cacophony around us.

The Spontaneous Inner Voice of Conscience

But how does conscience achieve this synthesis? As Samuel Taylor Coleridge explained and explored in various ways over his long career, moral imagination arises in consciousness spontaneously, appearing as the "still, small voice," a soft voice easily ignored. The spontaneous is an intermediate operation of human will. It's flanked on one side by the free will (by what we autonomously choose to acknowledge as both true and personally relevant to ourselves or to the situation we are struggling with) and on the other side by the passive or receptive will (which is what's true about our situation whether we like it or not—the intransigent facts of the situation. These are realities that, like primary sense data, impinge upon us inescapably).

To say that conscience operates spontaneously, then, is to say conscience is where all of received wisdom and all of my own knowledge of my own situation get assembled into a single, morally meaningful pattern. In simple situations, it's easy to see what to do. In heartbreakingly complicated situations, it's not.

In difficult situations, we may need both to survey repeatedly whatever wisdom we can find and to examine again every detail and every assumption we are making about our own situations. As we do so, conscience steadily guides us. Conscience does so, Christianity teaches, by aligning the goodness within us to whatever goodness is accessible within the situation we face. Conscience helps us to become conscious of the alignment of those two magnets, so that we can feel ourselves pulled toward what is for us the morally right choice to make.

When the creative, imaginative process of conscientious discernment reaches its conclusion, that shows up as the inward conviction "this is what I should do here." Tradition teaches that as the magnets are aligned there is a release of tension or a lessening of anxiety. The sign of successful discernment, Christian tradition teaches, is that we feel at peace with our decision even though we may also feel deeply sad. Wait to implement a decision, tradition teaches, to see if this inner peace and steadfastness develops: do nothing under the pressure of an inner urgency. Inner urgency is a sign of unconscious pressure of some kind.

We are, of course, free to obey or to ignore the voice of conscience: nothing external compels us. Conscience is an inner voice. The spontaneity of conscience, the spontaneity of imagination speaking in the voice of conscience, is evident in how commonly we use variants on the passive voice in speaking of such decisions. "It occurred to me," we say. "It dawned on me that . . ."; "I was convinced that . . . ." Even people who are not in the least religious will say things like "I felt called to . . . ."

How do we get to such moments of moral clarity? Only through the intellectually and personally difficult work of living with the questions we can't answer. Only by living with moral conflicts for which there is no easy and obvious answer. Only by facing squarely the ambiguity and the paradox at the heart of human experience. We must seek wisdom we are afraid to find. We must look for facts we don't want to face. We have to consider points of view from which we would prefer to hide. We have to accept our moral responsibility both for our own well-being and to the well-being of others in a world replete with what appear to be zero-sum conflicts. It can be a painful process. Our only comfort is confidence that there is a genuine goodness at the core of us, confidence that we are loved, confidence that we do have a moral center deep within us, a moral compass we can rightly trust.

Conscience, Morality, and Politics

Conscience is just as important politically as it is personally. The moral imagination shapes the decision-making process in political matters just as it does for personal matters. It's all the same process, but employed now with a far wider range of data and seeking the common good of the entire community. What Martin Luther King Jr. said in 1965 is even more true fifty years later:

> What we are facing today is the fact that through our scientific and technological genius we've made of this world a neighborhood. And now through our moral and ethical commitment we must make of it a brotherhood. We must all learn to live together as brothers—or we will all perish together as fools. This is the great issue facing us today. No individual can live alone; no nation can live alone; We are tied together.[1]

Acting *in good conscience* can keep us from perishing together as fools, which seems to be the path we are on together at the moment.

Making political decisions *in good conscience* is no small challenge. Collaboration is crucial, because none of us understand the common good in its entirety. We have only a partial grasp of the experience and the needs of people whose lives are quite different from our own. Furthermore, in public matters decisions cannot be based upon appeals to religious authority. They must be based upon public facts and rigorous analysis of public facts. In the Christian humanist vision, that's not a problem: my religious faith assures me that the best facts will always point us in the best direction. The right solution to a problem will be "right" in both senses of the word: both reasonably based on good data and morally correct.

On complex problems—climate policy, for instance—adjudicating and juggling multiple perspectives will be a major creative task. Good governance is always a major creative task, which is to say governance requires the incessant revising that informs the working life of any artist, musician, or writer. In the arts communities, everyone knows that nobody gets it right on the first try. Artists also know that the voices of demonic judgmentalism serve only to derail creative momentum. But in the current political climate, legislation or policy that fails to be flawless will reliably be denounced as damned and shameful.

Worse yet, "government" itself is declared to be the problem—as if living in a failed state would be better for all of us. When democratic self-governance is declared the villain, when honest and honorable contribution to the common good is denounced as "theft," it's time to ask what the alternatives are. Who else will run

---

1. King, "Remaining Awake Through a Great Revolution."

the country? Will we turn the government over to lobbyists? Who profits from destroying community, dismantling the common good, and setting us at one another throats?

I worry that creative and morally responsible governance has lost out to the political equivalent of gang warfare, us versus them, the saved versus the damned. Rigid ideologues are consumed with contempt, derision, and outrage; courtesy, inclusivity, and hospitality seem to be lost causes. As a result, nothing gets done. Creative, morally sensitive, incremental, and recursive problem-solving is no longer possible.

And that's catastrophic: intelligent creative collaboration is in everyone's best interests. It's also in our biological nature as brainy social obligates: this is how we survive *and how we have always survived*. If we are going to continue to survive, both as a nation and as a species—if we hope for a fate better than dying together as fools—we must reclaim the common ground of intelligent, morally responsible problem-solving. We must reclaim conscience as a creative process. With sufficient moral imagination and a firm commitment to acting in good conscience, the good that is available within us and among us and around us can rise gradually into harmony, into a harmony that my tradition unabashedly calls *holy*.

Is Conscience Accurate?

Here's a crucial detail to keep in mind: the spontaneously arising moral judgment is not *by virtue of its spontaneity alone* necessarily correct. (That was the overwhelming error of German Romanticism. It's also the error of the sincere pedophile, the sincere Nazi, the sincere suicide bomber.) Everything depends upon the input, because imagination is a perceptual process. Here as elsewhere in life, it's garbage in, garbage out. And so we need experts of every kind, from scholars who have read all forty-six volumes of Augustine of Hippo to the folks who know how to fit running shoes. They are also fallible, of course. But the human ability to learn from one another is one of the great keys to our evolutionary success. If you are not willing to learn from other people, you will make avoidable mistakes.

Our lives are already beset by far too many avoidable mistakes. Let's not add to the toll.

Here's another notable detail. Nothing in the Christian discernment process gets us to universally applicable law we can impose upon others in a rigidly authoritarian manner. If the inputs are honest and careful, if the inputs are thoughtful and as accurate as we can make them, then conscience can bring an individual to conclusions whose moral rectitude is as reliable as life allows. But that's all. If I do the intellectual and personal work I have to do, and if I do that work with a focused non-attachment to the petty preferences of ego or social prestige or what have you, then my conscience can prompt me toward what I should do, or away from what I should avoid. Tradition insists that this is my surest path to finding the wisdom and the peace of mind and the moral maturity I seek in life. Tradition insists that engaging this process is necessary for spiritual and moral maturity.

But note: that doesn't tell me anything about what choices you should make on your path toward spiritual and moral maturity. Only your own moral imagination—your own conscience—can lead you along. You must listen carefully for that still small voice in your heart.

And yet, keep your common sense plugged in. Condemnation has its place in a society. We need the law. The law is fallible and it's always a work in progress. But the law represents our best, mutual, rational effort to articulate standards of behavior necessary to the common good of the whole society. If it doesn't, or where it fails, the law must be revised—not abandoned. What is moral is a much higher standard than what is legal; we are struggling here to understand morality, not to understand the law. Confusing the moral with the legal is one of the core mistakes of theocracy. As I see it, morality cannot be imposed. But the law by definition is always imposed, even though (ideally) it is imposed by a democratically elected government and on the basis of significant consensus.

Ultimately, the formation of the good conscience is a circular process: if we seek a "well-formed conscience" (as it is called), if we listen carefully to that still small voice within, if regularly we obey our own conscientious promptings, then over time we will more clearly hear what the voice of conscience has to say to us. In this way, conscience both seeks and is shaped by the morally authentic good life in all of its imaginative particularity. Only by living virtuously do we come to understand both the virtue we seek and the virtue about which the sages speak. And the same is true of democracy: only by struggling to live together wisely do we discover the wisdom we need to live together wisely. Only by wise compromise do we discover the wisdom about the common good that only compromise can reveal. I said earlier that Christianity is a religion for grown-ups. Democracy is a politics for grown-ups.

Let me repeat: this is a densely creative process. As any musician will tell you, the only way to learn to play the violin is by playing the violin. The only way to become a poet is by writing poetry. And the only way to live in good conscience is by endeavoring to live in good conscience with all that it entails. Neither life nor morality is an exercise in theory—that's where both the absolutists and the nihilists go wrong. The absolutists pretend to have an iron-clad theory, and the nihilists reply your theory has no clothes, but slowly I've come to understand that moral wisdom is not a theory. Moral wisdom is a creative process.

Conscience and Moral Autonomy

My account of conscience conflicts with any authoritarian version of organized Christianity. It also conflicts with radical claims that all of us are totally depraved. I certainly grew up knowing that at least some Catholics believed that to have a "well-formed conscience" meant that one understood and accepted the absolute truth of whatever the bishops were saying. And at least some bishops demanded that deference, as did some parish clergy. Not the best of them, I suppose; but enough to give the institution as a whole its reputation for rigidity.

But these radical denials of conscience are malignant distortions of the larger tradition. At one point years ago I was both startled and charmed to discover that Thomas Aquinas himself—historically speaking, the magisterial figure in Catholic theology—that Aquinas himself had defended the autonomy of the individual conscience. He flatly insisted that difficult decisions can't be made in the abstract by remote authorities laying down absolute rules. Difficult decisions must be left to the good conscience of the people closest to the situation, he argued. Only they have the fullest possible command of all the intuitive realities at hand. Only they have a full grasp of all the complex, elusive variables shaping the problem. The only unquestionable moral wrong, Aquinas concluded, was the failure to obey one's own conscience. Thomas Aquinas said that in the 1200s.[2]

More recently, Pope Francis seemed to be channeling Aquinas in his correspondence with Eugenio Scalfari, co-founder and former editor of the Italian newspaper *La Repubblica*. In a letter published in the paper on July 7, 2013, Scalfari, an atheist, asked the pope about the church's attitude to nonbelievers. Pope Francis replied, "the issue for the unbeliever lies in obeying his or her conscience. There is sin, even for those who have no faith, when conscience is not followed. Listening to and obeying conscience means deciding on the fact of what is understood to be good or evil. It on the basis of this choice that the goodness or evil of actions is determined."[3] Needless to say, such claims undercut authoritarian American bishops trying to impose upon even upon non-Catholics their own opposition to birth control. It will be interesting to watch this conflict play out within Catholicism, because Francis's position reflects the distinctively Catholic position that that the image of God within each of us remains indelible.

Conscience has drawn me where I never imagined going, eliciting abilities I never dreamed I had in me. That's probably true for all of us. One way or another, conscience generates whatever meaning a meaningful life has. But through all of it, my decision-making has been framed two bits of advice I happily hand along.

First, one must be especially careful in contradicting the beliefs long upheld by the many and the wise: the high intellectual standards

---

2. Aquinas, *Summa Theologica* (Ia, IIae, 94a:1–4) 286–288.
3. Pope Francis, "Letter to a Non-Believer."

of "in good conscience" can keep any of us from making devastating mistakes. (Embarrassing mistakes are another matter. The angel in charge of preventing that is seriously negligent.)

Second, an error of long standing does not by virtue of its longevity become true. The high personal standards of "in good conscience"—the demand for self-knowledge—can shine a very bright light on the shadows of error or self-deception. That's how Christians came to lead the campaigns against slavery and, later, against racial segregation and an illegal war. That's how Ireland, one of the most Catholic nations on earth, in May of 2015 defied both certain biblical verses and its own bishops to become the first nation legalizing gay marriage in a popular referendum: good conscience is the court of last resort.

In the end, we are morally obligated to act always in good conscience within the details of a given situation. Nothing more, nothing less. It seems to me that if the good really were "just an opinion," none of us would wake up spontaneously at 3 a.m. agonizing over what to do. We would be able to do whatever we want much more casually. We are awakened in part by a yearning for some aspect of the good that we have not yet made fully conscious. Or we are awakened by questions, because making a choice in good conscience involves facing every hard question. Or we are awakened by a judgmental inner voice—the voice of shame—that can berate and belittle us mercilessly.

As a Christian humanist, all I can do in life is to seek good answers to good questions trusting above all to the realities of love, compassion, and wisdom. All I can do is seek the answers I need, trusting that the good that is in me may be calling me to a deeper wisdom and a richer joy than I can yet imagine.

Conscience, Confidence, and Resilience to Shame

The blessing available here, tradition teaches, is that a decision made in good conscience is not followed by an exhausting round of second-guessing and regrets. For centuries now, Christian spiritual wisdom has taught that this inner relief, this abiding self-confidence, is potent evidence that even the most painful decision was in fact made in good conscience.

That's been true in my experience. It has been remarkably true. It is for me the deepest "proof," were proof possible, that conscience is real and it really counts for something very serious. I'm convinced that the conscience as a creative process is our best guide to a life shaped by moral wisdom, authenticity, honesty, compassion, responsibility, and so forth.

And, needless to say, a decision I've made *in good conscience* leaves me much more resilient to shame. I am less vulnerable to the crass condemnations of people who have not a clue what's behind the choices I have made in my life. And I'm less vulnerable in a way that's neither defensive nor egotistical because if I *have* made a mistake, at least I know it was an honest mistake. There's nothing shameful about honest mistakes. We are not bad people nor morally inadequate because we are not perfect. That was the temptation in the garden: thinking that we have to be perfect and furthermore perfectly in control in order to be good.

Christianity at its best is not about easy escape from the moral complexity of life. At its best, it offers nuanced and often ancient resources for coping honestly with that complexity. At its best, the doctrine of conscience allows for a networked, distributed moral intelligence. Like other networked endeavors, including democracy, networked moral intelligence is imperfect. But it's better than the alternatives. Over time, conscientious Christians have wisely adapted to cultural change by rereading the Christian moral heritage in the light of new facts or diverse cultural contexts. In the name of conscience, Christians have confronted even long-tolerated evils such as slavery, racism, homophobia, and the oppression of women. In the name of conscience, Christians have confronted evil both within the church and within the culture, calling for necessary change. Conscience can do all this without giving way either to mindless totalitarian absolutes or to the normal nihilism of isolated individualists.

Conscience thus understood cannot be weaponized. It cannot be turned into a basis for condemning others wholesale. It cannot without self-contradiction be used to deny the innate moral dignity of others or to coerce their behavior. *But by the same measure, it is accountable to the well-being of others.* The divine within me must be within you and within everything or none of this works. That's why appeals to conscience are not a covert form of "anything goes."

Conscience is never "just an opinion." It gives me an answer to that question, *how do you know?* Let me tell you, I might reply: here is all the evidence and all the analysis of evidence that I have considered. And if you have reached a different conclusion, share with me your evidence and your reasoning and above all your stories about your own life. We can rethink this issue together, knowing that nothing either of us can do will get the discussion to inerrancy or infallibility about one another's lives and one another's choices. None of us know for sure.

Don't trust those snakes saying otherwise.

13

Postscript: What I Should Have Said to My Son

So what should I have said to my son that morning? Easy. (Or easy to see now, at a distance of decades.) I should have said, "At lunch today, ask them why they don't eat what they don't eat. What's the point?"

We might have had an interesting conversation over dinner that night, because the rules to which his friends referred are part of the formation of conscience within different traditions. Muslims fast during Ramadan that they might personally understand the hunger of the poor. During that month, they require themselves to donate to the poor—not to programming or building upkeep or clergy salaries within their own religious congregations, but directly to the poor.

Jews don't eat pork, or other ritually "unclean" foods, in recognition of the fact that evil permeates all of reality, an evil made manifest symbolically in animals or fish that are unusual in some way. Most fish have gills, scales, and fins, for instance. Shellfish don't. Shellfish thus symbolize deviation from moral ideals. If we are called to the good, then we need to avoid evil at every level—and that means recognizing it when it shows up and resisting what "everyone else" is doing. That's a very complex lesson made concrete enough to teach a child: there's wisdom for you!

POSTSCRIPT: WHAT I SHOULD HAVE SAID TO MY SON

Hindus are vegetarians and sometimes vegans because it is wrong to bring suffering to any sentient creature. If it is wrong to cause suffering to a chicken, surely it is wrong to taunt a classmate: try that message on for size if you are a school principal! Factory farms, anybody? Slave factories in China? What about war? What about the cruelties of ordinary office politics or attack ads during political campaigns? What about the suffering caused by pollution and unwise development? "Do not cause suffering to a sentient creature" may be an impossibly high moral norm, but that's what moral norms are for. How to live out such an ideals is complex, but we can begin by living it out in whatever small way comes to hand—like not eating meat or not ridiculing a classmate. A morally sensitive conscience will then begin to find other ways as well.

Catholic abstinence from meat on Friday—a rule officially dropped in the 1960s, but more recently revived as a spiritual practice—argues that if Jesus died in solidarity with the poor and oppressed, then on the day on which he died we should at the very least refrain from luxury. In the European Middle Ages, when this spiritual practice arose, meat was a luxury: only the very wealthiest ate meat regularly. That's still true in much of the world today. Furthermore, the word "meat" originally meant food of any kind—not simply animal flesh. Fasting, in short, was a spiritual practice aimed directly at the socioeconomic elite, who were the only people who ever had enough to eat.

And so—what if, once a week, we all fasted in some way or other in deliberate, intentional solidarity with all of those who are hungry? Like the Ramadan fast, that could make a difference over time. Not necessarily, of course. None of this happens necessarily, mechanically, mindlessly. It's an art. The arts are exercises in intentionality.

Morally intentional eating practices are one way, one spiritual practice, intended to change how we experience the world. They are a practical poetry, an embodied poetry, which can inform the moral imagination. What one eats or does not eat matters far less than taking seriously the depth and extent of our obligations to other human beings. What to eat or not to eat surely is a matter of "opinion," which can be a way of naming distinctive human cultures. But the fact that we are obligated to the common good is an absolutely central moral truth—a truth to which each of these good kids would easily have agreed. In good humanist fashion, they would have done so without forcing their own cultural-religious traditions and practices upon anyone else.

If I had not snapped at him as I did, my son might have learned something about the formation of conscience: Listen to your friends. Ask questions. Let them question you. Continue to be the kind of guy who is friends with people whose background is different from yours. Be glad that at your school Jews and Muslims and Hindus and Christians have lunch together every day as ordinary good friends—both men and women, both recent immigrants and the great-grandchildren of immigrants. Never take that for granted: the difference between right and wrong begins right there, with seeing the common humanity we all share. Cherish these friends with whom you sometimes play Dungeons & Dragons and sometimes talk about moral issues of remarkable complexity. How should we live? What matters most in life? How are we going to achieve that set of goals?

Christianity as I understand it says we can face such questions fearlessly, openly, listening to others, confident that the image of God dwells in each of us, good calling to good inexorably.

Bibliography

Alexander, Michelle. *The New Jim Crow: Mass Incarceration in the Age of Colorblindness*. New York: Free Press, 2012.
Aquinas, Thomas. *Summa Theologica: A Concise Translation*. Edited by Timothy McDermott. Allen, TX: Christian Classics, 1989.
Bellah, Robert N., Richard Madsen, William M. Sullivan, Ann Swidler, and Steven M. Tipton. *Habits of the Heart: Individualism and Commitment in American Life*. New York: Harper & Row, 1985.
Brach, Tara. *Radical Acceptance: Embracing Your Life with the Heart of a Buddha*. New York: Bantam, 2003.
Brock, Rita Nakashima, and Rebecca Ann Parker. *Proverbs of Ashes: Violence, Redemptive Suffering, and the Search for What Saves Us*. Boston: Beacon, 2001.
———. *Saving Paradise: How Christianity Traded Love of This World for Crucifixion and Empire*. Boston: Beacon, 2008.
Brown, Brené. *The Gifts of Imperfection: Let Go of Who You Think You're Supposed to Be and Embrace Who You Are*. Center City, MN: Hazelden, 2010.
———. *I Thought It Was Just Me: Women Reclaiming Power and Courage in a Culture of Shame*. New York: Gotham, 2010.
Chödrön, Pema. *Getting Unstuck: Breaking Your Habitual Patterns and Encountering Naked Reality*. Audio recording, 2005. http://www.soundstrue.com/store/getting-unstuck-3900.html
Cox, Harvey. "The Market as God." *The Atlantic*, March 1999. Reprinted in *The Best Christian Writing 2000*, edited by John Wilson, 64–78. San Francisco: HarperSanFrancisco, 2000. http://www.theatlantic.com/magazine/archive/1999/03/the-market-as-god/306397/.
Dalai Lama. *Beyond Religion: Ethics for the Whole World*. New York: Houghton Mifflin Harcourt, 2011.
———. *Toward a True Kinship of Faiths: How the World's Religions Can Come Together*. New York: Doubleday, 2010.
De Waal, Frans. *Primates and Philosophers: How Morality Evolves*. Princeton: Princeton University Press, 2006.

Eagleton, Terry. *Reason, Faith, and Revolution: Reflections on the God Debate.* The Terry Lectures. New Haven: Yale University Press, 2009.

Edwards, James C. *The Plain Sense of Things: The Fate of Religion in an Age of Normal Nihilism.* University Park, PA: The Pennsylvania State University Press, 1997.

Edwards, Jonathan. "Sinners in the Hands of an Angry God." *The Norton Anthology of American Literature,* Volume 1. Edited by Ronald Gottesman, Laurence B. Holland, David Kalstone, Francis Murphy, Hershel Parker, and William H. Pritchard. New York: Norton, 1979.

Gottschall, Jonathan. *The Storytelling Animal: How Stories Make Us Human.* Boston: Houghton Mifflin Harcourt, 2012.

Graeber, David. *Debt: The First Five Thousand Years.* New York: Melville House, 2011.

Haidt, Jonathan. *The Happiness Hypothesis.* New York: Basic, 2006.

Heyrman, Christine Leigh. *Southern Cross: The Beginnings of the Bible Belt.* New York: Knopf, 1997.

Hyde, Lewis. *The Gift: Creativity and the Artist in the Modern World.* 2nd ed. New York: Vintage, 2007.

Iacoboni, Marco. *Mirroring People: The New Science of How We Connect With Others.* New York: Farrar, Straus and Giroux, 2008.

Kagan, Jerome. *Three Seductive Ideas.* Cambridge, MA: Harvard University Press, 1998.

Kearney, Richard. *Anatheism: Returning to God After God.* New York: Columbia University Press, 2010.

King, Martin Luther, Jr. "Remaining Awake Through a Great Revolution." Commencement Address for Oberlin College, June 1965. http://www.oberlin.edu/external/EOG/BlackHistoryMonth/MLK/CommAddress.html.

Küng, Hans, and Karl-Josef Kuschel. *A Global Ethic: The Declaration of the Parliament of the World's Religions.* New York: Continuum, 1998.

Lynch, Michael P. *True to Life: Why Truth Matters.* Cambridge: MIT Press, 2005.

Martin, William. *With God on Our Side: The Rise of the Religious Right in America.* New York: Broadway, 2005.

McAdams, Dan P. *The Stories We Live By: Personal Myths and the Making of the Self.* New York: Guilford, 1993.

McFarland, Thomas. *Coleridge and the Pantheist Tradition.* New York: Oxford University Press, 1969.

Miles, Jack. *Christ: A Crisis in the Life of God.* New York: Alfred A. Knopf, 2001.

———. *God: A Biography.* New York: Knopf, 1995.

Pope Francis. "Letter to a Non-Believer," 4 September 2013. https://w2.vatican.va/content/francesco/en/letters/2013/documents/papa-francesco20130911eugenio-scalfari.html.

Prickett, Stephen. *Narrative, Religion, and Science: Fundamentalism Versus Irony, 1700-1999.* New York: Cambridge University Press, 2002.

BIBLIOGRAPHY

Sacks, Jonathan. *The Dignity of Difference: How to Avoid the Clash of Civilizations*. London and New York: Continuum, 2002.

Salzberg, Sharon. *Faith: Trusting Your Own Deepest Experience*. New York: Riverhead, 2002.

Schank, Roger C. *Tell Me a Story: Narrative and Intelligence*. 1990; rpt. Evanston, IL: Northwestern University Press, 1995.

Schweitzer, Friedrich L. *The Postmodern Life Cycle: Challenges for Church and Theology*. St. Louis: Chalice, 2004.

Stockitt, Robin. *Restoring the Shamed: Toward a Theology of Shame*. Eugene, OR: Wipf and Stock, 2012.

Taylor, Charles. *A Secular Age*. Cambridge, MA: Belknap Press of Harvard University Press, 2007.

Tickle, Phyllis A. *God-Talk in America*. New York: Crossroad, 1997.

Toulmin, Stephen. *Return to Reason*. Cambridge MA: Harvard University Press, 2001.

Wallace, Catherine M. *For Fidelity: How Intimacy and Commitment Enrich Our Lives*. New York: Knopf, 1998.

———. *Motherhood in the Balance: Children, Career, God, and Me*. Harrisburg, PA: Morehouse, 2000.

———. *Selling Ourselves Short: Why We Struggle to Earn a Living and Have a Life*. Grand Rapids, MI: Brazos, 2003.

White, L. Michael. *Scripting Jesus: The Gospels in Rewrite*. New York: Harper One, 2010.

Wordsworth, William. *Poetical Works*. Ed. Thomas Hutchinson. New ed., revised by Ernest De Selincourt. London: Oxford University Press, 1936.

www.ingramcontent.com/pod-product-compliance
Lightning Source LLC
Chambersburg PA
CBHW022125160426
43197CB00009B/1162